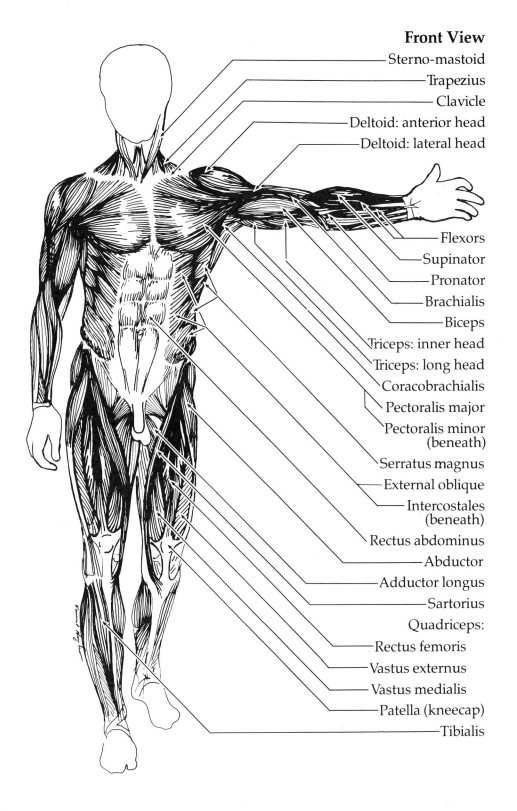

Front View

Sterno-mastoid

Trapezius

Clavicle

Deltoid: anterior head

Deltoid: lateral head

Flexors

Supinator

Pronator

Brachialis

Biceps

Triceps: inner head

Triceps: long head

Coracobrachialis

Pectoralis major

Pectoralis minor
(beneath)

Serratus magnus

External oblique

Intercostales
(beneath)

Rectus abdominus

Abductor

Adductor longus

Sartorius

Quadriceps:

Rectus femoris

Vastus externus

Vastus medialis

Patella (kneecap)

Tibialis

Rear View

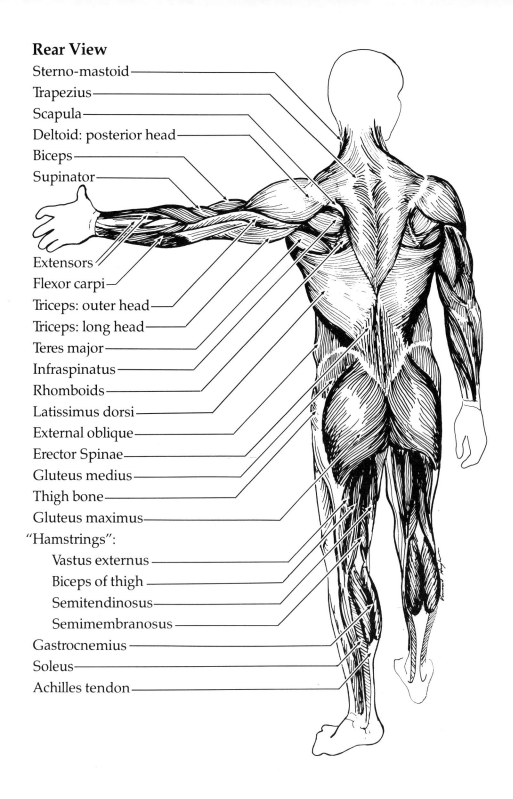

Sterno-mastoid

Trapezius

Scapula

Deltoid: posterior head

Biceps

Supinator

Extensors

Flexor carpi

Triceps: outer head

Triceps: long head

Teres major

Infraspinatus

Rhomboids

Latissimus dorsi

External oblique

Erector Spinae

Gluteus medius

Thigh bone

Gluteus maximus

"Hamstrings":

    Vastus externus

    Biceps of thigh

    Semitendinosus

    Semimembranosus

Gastrocnemius

Soleus

Achilles tendon

Prime Cut

Prime Cut

TOTAL FITNESS
FOR MEN 18 TO 34

PETE BROCCOLETTI

ICARUS PRESS
South Bend, Indiana

PRIME CUT
Copyright © 1983 by Pete Broccoletti

Icarus Press, Inc.
Post Office Box 1225
South Bend, Indiana 46624

1   2   3   4   5   6   87   86   85   84   83

Library of Congress Cataloging in Publication Data

Broccoletti, Pete, 1942–
    Prime cut.

    Includes index.
    1. Weight lifting. 2. Physical fitness for men.
3. Nutrition. I. Title.
GV546.B77 1983   613.7'044   83–12984
ISBN 0–89651–604–0
ISBN 0–89651–605–9 (wire-bound)

A special word of thanks to Stan Jones, the defensive line coach of the Denver Broncos. Stan was not only a great all-pro and coach but a dedicated weight lifter who trained at York, Pennsylvania, and with the great Clyde Emerich, strength coach of the Chicago Bears, while Stan played for the Bears. He has been an inspiration and a lot of help. Thanks also to Rob Lytle and Dave Preston of the Broncos, who graciously agreed to pose for their pictures contained herein when I was working for the Denver Broncos. Their fine physiques should be an inspiration to all of you.

Thanks also go to Stuart S. Kerxton of Warrenton, Virginia, who shot many of the pictures, and to Brian Thomas for the use of his Spartan Gym in Merryfield, Virginia. I appreciate the patience of Pete Colwell, Chris Sluss, Tim Bassett, Curt Davis, Mike Scott, and Arn Kritsky in posing for the hundreds of pictures we shot and for the time delay in getting this book out. Thanks to Gene Paskiet, the all-time great Notre Dame football trainer. His dedication to the young men of Notre Dame and to the University is an inspiration.

Last but not least thanks go to my dear friend, Rafael Guerrero, for the use of his Gold Coast Gyms in Ft. Lauderdale, Florida, and his continued advice and support.

INTRODUCTION

PRIME CUT connotes lean, juicy meat with little fat, and that is the condition men 18–34 should be in. They should be fit, tight, with life's forces percolating through their body. And that's where the title for this book comes in: the models I have chosen for it all exemplify a prime cut of manhood!

That 30-inch waistline you used to have, did you ever really think you'd be able to keep it after high school without working at it? Perhaps during college you could, by keeping on the go, playing ball, racing to classes, going out on dates, generally running through the most exciting part of your life. And in so doing, you burned up lots of calories and kept in shape. But it doesn't take long, when you stop doing those things, for it to show. That particularly explains why that late-night sub, pizza or beer magically appears in an expanded waistline or behind, and why your clothes from school seem too small or don't fit at all.

Levi has a great ad out that also is a good selling point for this book: "I don't care if you can bench press 200 pounds before breakfast and run five miles, you're still not in the shape you were in when you were 18. That's why Levi makes Levi's for men with a scotch more room in the thighs."

Major physiological changes occur in you at about 12, 18, and 35. After your teens your metabolism slows down. Remember, you are at the peak of your sexual drive at 19, while a woman doesn't reach her peak till 38. As you pass your teens your testosterone level, which helps build muscle in the man, continues to drop. Because of the slowing down of your metabolism, as you grow older your body fat seems to accumulate easier. Therefore, in order to keep a tight body you need to either change your diet or increase your exercise. Better than that is a combination: exercise and proper diet. But since you generally do not have the time to do all the sports you would like to, you have to be more selective in utilizing it, both in terms of what you most enjoy and what will be most effective in keeping you fit.

One of the major reasons I have written so many books on weight training, conditioning, and sports (including *Shape Up for Soccer; Building Up; 35 and Holding; The Notre Dame Weight-Training Program for Football,* also *The Notre Dame Weight-Training Program for Baseball, Hockey, Wrestling, and Your Body*) is not to give specialized programs just for different sports, but also for different age brackets, programs that take into account the changes in a person's physiology and life-style. At this point in your life you are probably finished with school and starting your career. You may be starting a family and most likely are attempting to lead a satisfying social life, in the midst of everything else. Married men don't generally worry too much about their appearance; they have caught their mate and are content until, after a few years of marriage, they suddenly look at themselves in the mirror and think, How did I get to this state? Now you have got your work cut out for you: getting on the right diet, and exercise. It's not as easy to stay disciplined and get back in shape as it is for the single man, who has more time and is more motivated to keep himself attractive to partners. But maintaining your health is ample motivation, no matter whether you're married or single. Remember that the best way to prevent a heart attack is to keep body fat in check and give your heart a good workout with some cardiovascular conditioning a few times a week.

There is no other sport you can participate in that will make you look better faster than weight training. There is no sport that can build muscles as well as weight training. There is hardly any other sport that you can participate in in some form almost till the day you die than weight training. I trained under a priest at Notre Dame (Father Lange), who trained till he was 80! Consider also the physiological effects of weight training and general conditioning: when you look better, you feel better. Looking better also helps build up your confidence, which is important not just for your social life but in dealing with clients, patients, customers, and your peers, and this in turn helps you get new jobs and new accounts, assuring you of a better future. Ask yourself these questions: Does the way you look deter you from seeking a promotion of a new job? Does your out-of-shape appearance hurt your performance in the courtroom or your sales pitch? Don't you think that shaping up will help get you more dates if you're single or, if you are married, that it will rekindle some excitement in your mate? Whether you are too skinny and want to build up or too heavy and want to slim down, or whether you just want to get in shape and tighten up, this book will do more for you than any other book on the market. Besides nutrition, diet, flexibility, and weight training, I have included chapters on aerobics to get your heart in shape and afford you some fun, as well as an important chapter on how to choose your club or gym. Joining a club is an important and expensive step, this book is worth its price for that chapter alone!

As a word of caution, I recommend before you start exercising that you get a complete physical from your doctor, plus a stress test. You should specifically ask him if there are any limits on your weight-training or aerobic activity. Be sure to bring up any old injuries you might have had, and check them out. Then I recommend one month of progressive calisthenics, sit-ups, leg raises, push-ups, and chin-ups if you haven't been training in the last year. An ounce of prevention is worth a pound of cure, and it's better to go slowly in getting into your new regime than chance injuring yourself by going hog-wild at first.

NUTRITION

Now that you are starting to exercise and get in shape again, the subject of nutrition should mean more to you than memories of your mother's homecooked meals. You need nutrients to give you the energy to exercise, repair muscle tissue, and promote muscle growth. Two hours of daily exercise every week will not guarantee significant results if you don't eat correctly. "You are what you eat," warned the well-known nutritionist, Adelle Davis. Because the physical composition and condition of your body is determined by your diet, you must initiate good health practices in your kitchen.

Following an unbalanced diet will only lead to development of vitamin or mineral deficiencies that could result in illness or at least poor skin condition, fatigue, and irritability. If you eat a large amount of junk food, such as soda pop, potato chips, cookies, cake, and candy, you will most likely be overweight and have high blood pressure, assuring you prime candidacy for heart disease. You will also probably experience the "lows"—depression after your sugar high.

Despite the popularity of health-food stores, your patronage of them does not necessarily assure good personal nutrition. Unfortunately, the food you buy in a health-food store might not be any better than that bought in a conventional grocery store. Only careful selection of health foods will steer you away from wasting your money or gaining a false sense of security from eating that food. However, some products in such stores are healthier than those purchased elsewhere. Some examples are: specially prepared whole wheat bread, homemade yogurt, and fruit and vegetables organically grown rather than dosed with possibly harmful chemicals.

Fresh fruits and vegetables provide more minerals and vitamins than those that are frozen or canned. Steaming your vegetables rather than boiling them retains nutrients. Like junk food, white or American bread should be avoided because the flour is too processed. I recommend French, Italian, whole wheat—which is the best for you—rye or pumpernickel. Because all sugars are empty calories, they should be

5

avoided if possible. They also give you an artificial high which results in a crash. Allow your body to obtain the natural sugar or fructose from the fruits you eat, rather than from sugar added to your coffee or cereal. If you need a sweetener, use an artificial sweetener (carefully read that label, however!). Surprise your system at your usual junk-food session. Try snacking on nutritional food like yogurt, with a few teaspoons of wheat germ mixed in. Or try some anchovies, sardines (with the oil washed off) or cheese on wheat thins.

The adult male needs about 2500 calories daily of well-balanced meals to grow and function properly. The foods needed include proteins, fats, carbohydrates, mineral salts, vitamins, and water. Generally, your diet—not a weight gain or loss diet—should consist of 60% carbohydrates, 25% protein, and 15% fats.

PROTEIN

As the body's primary building material and the basis for living cells, protein is very important to weight-trained athletes. Your brain, organs, eyes, muscles, skin, hair, and nails are composed of protein. Additionally, your body's defense mechanisms, antibodies that fight infection, are also protein. Protein is the key both to the repair of muscle tissue and to its growth. When you lift weights rigorously you break down muscle tissue. This breakdown is known as *catabolism; anabolism* is the growth and repair of the muscle tissue. Anabolism must exceed catabolism to build larger, stronger muscles.

The best sources of protein—eggs, milk, dairy products, meat, fish— are complete: they contain all eight essential amino acids, the building blocks of protein. Of the twenty-two different amino acids known and needed in forming tissues, all but eight are manufactured in the human body. Those eight must therefore be supplied in our food. They are: tryptophane, lysine, methionine, phenylalanine, threonine, valine, leucine, and isoleucine.

Many differences of opinion exist as to how much protein an individual needs daily. The National Research Council in Washington, D.C., recommends 0.42 grams per pound of body weight. Others, particularly bodybuilders, recommend much higher amounts—because more protein is needed for both muscle repair and muscle growth in weight lifters. Bigger muscles would necessitate more protein. For those of you who are becoming involved in weight lifting or simply aiming toward your body tone of college days, I think one-half gram of protein per body pound weight is sufficient. A little excess protein is harmless. You will excrete what your body doesn't need.

The following is a basic chart for protein counting:

Food	Serving	Protein Gram Count
eggs	1	6 grams
milk	8 oz.	8 grams
cheese	1 oz.	4 grams
beans	½ cup	6–9 grams
cottage cheese	1 oz.	4 grams
yogurt	8 oz.	8 grams
liver	3 oz.	24 grams
tuna fish	3 oz.	24 grams
chicken	3 oz.	24 grams
steak	3 oz.	23 grams
ham	3 oz.	15 grams
pork chops	3 oz.	15 grams
brewer's yeast	1 oz.	12 grams
wheat germ	1 oz.	8 grams

As the chart indicates, some meats have a higher protein count and are more beneficial. Liver, which might not appeal to some of you, is tremendously rich in protein, vitamins, and minerals.

I am also recommending eggs on my protein chart. One of nature's best foods, eggs are a valuable source of protein; they contain the vitamins A, B, and D, in addition to important unsaturated fats. Eggs contain lecithin, a homogenizing agent that breaks down fat into minuscule particles that can pass readily into the tissue.

Yet eggs contain cholesterol, the so-called contributing factor in arteriosclerosis and heart disease. As we hover near the age of thirty, we have been warned regularly to significantly reduce or eliminate our cholesterol intake. Recent studies question past statements on cholesterol. In fact, a new study has shown that a lack of cholesterol can contribute to cancer. The long and short of this is that you should consult your doctor, be tuned in for new scientific truths, not just theories, and use your common sense. Don't completely cut out cholesterol. Limit it sensibly by cutting down on unnecessary fats that are high on cholesterol —like salad dressings, olive oil, and mayonnaise.

Probably the best way to answer the egg question, if you are overweight or have heart problems, is to consult your doctor about their use. For the rest of you, at least twelve eggs weekly should supply you with needed protein as well as vitamins and minerals. On the milk topic, I would recommend following the same precautions for overweight individuals or those with heart conditions. For the others, eight to sixteen ounces of low-fat or skim milk per day would be a good boost to your diet. However, if you are on a special diet like the Scarsdale Medical Diet, you may be required to forgo all dairy products while you attempt to lose weight (see below).

FATS

Fats are essential to good health maintenance because of their various functions within the body. Fat forms part of every cell, helps regulate water balance, allows important intestinal bacteria to multiply, forms sex and adrenal hormones, transports vitamins A, D, E, and K to the cells, and acts as a homogenizing agent that permits tiny fat and cholesterol particles (see *Protein*, above) into the tissues. The foods that are high in the essential fatty acids are avocados, nuts, French dressing, salad oil, cottonseed oil, and mayonnaise. If you have a deficiency in fatty acids, you might experience bloatedness, fatigue, sterility, loss of sex interest, or be overweight or underweight.

Remember my previous warnings about unnecessary cholesterol in specific foods, especially if you are overweight, on a diet, or have heart problems. Although I have listed the symptoms of a fatty-acid deficiency, most people need not worry about getting enough fatty acids in their diet; their chief concern is minimization of fat intake. However, do not be frightened by the word "fat." It is a rich energy source that will supply your body with valuable nutrients.

CARBOHYDRATES

Carbohydrates are best obtained through fruits and vegetables and not through concentrated calories like cookies, cake, candy, and other junk food. An often misjudged carbohydrate that has acquired a poor reputation is pasta. Spaghetti in its most common form, pasta is made from flour, eggs, and water, or just flour and water. Enriched pasta and spinach pasta are the most nutritional pasta. A small serving of spaghetti is only 155 calories with five grams of protein and thirty-two grams of carbohydrates. Pasta can provide stored-up energy. Long-distance runners often consume large quantities of pasta six hours or so before a race. Pasta sauce, however, contains anywhere from 100 to another 350 calories or more, especially if used generously. Many wasted calories are contained in your favorite marinara, ragu or meat sauce. If you dislike plain pasta, try adding a small amount of tomato sauce or a clam sauce as a substitution for a meat sauce. As an Italian-American, I can survive just so long without pasta, but I limit my use of sauce and avoid meat sauce entirely.

Carbohydrates, when ingested, break down into a simple sugar, glucose, which is used as a supply of energy. You generally need one-half gram of carbohydrates for each pound of body weight, but select your "carbs" from food sources which also supply lots of protein, minerals, and vitamins, such as cottage cheese, yogurt or enriched pasta. Bodybuilders and many dieters go on a zero- or low-carbohydrate diet for a cycle. Bodybuilders do it to "get cut up" (become defined). However, most realize some carbohydrates are needed to keep the energy level up. If you are interested in counting your calories and carbohydrates, I recommend Barbara Kraus's *Calories and Carbohydrates.*

Water and Fiber

Because the body and its muscles are comprised mostly of water, the health-conscious individual should be aware of its importance. The body utilizes water when it perspires as it cleanses itself from within. Drinking lots of water also flushes out your system of the poisons in certain foods. When possible, try to drink spring water, because of its richness in natural minerals and absence of additives.

Another necessary part of your diet is fiber, nature's laxative. It is the nondigestible part of food found in whole grains, nuts, fresh fruits, and vegetables. Interestingly, studies show that digestive problems do not occur, to a large extent, in civilizations that maintain high-fiber diets.

Vitamins

Getting into and staying in shape requires physical exercise, and physical exercise depletes the store of vital nutrients that are in the body. If the body is not supplied with necessary vitamins, the energy load will decrease and injuries may result. Vitamins, therefore, play a key role in good health.

I recommend supplements because so much of our food, especially at institutions, has the majority of vitamins and minerals boiled out. (Who can forget those lifeless vegetables on their college cafeteria trays?) Some doctors consider supplements to be a waste of money, but they do not take into account the lack of balanced meals most of us have, the loss of vitamins and minerals through food processing, nor the added demands on those individuals shaping up or in training.

Try these suggestions in your food preparation: steaming instead of boiling, baking in favor of frying, and simply eating raw fruits and vegetables rather than always cooking them.

The following is a list of vitamins and minerals with their recommended dosages:

Vitamin A necessary for eyesight as well as for normal cell growth, healthy skin, and skeletal development. It is found in green vegetables, carrots, apricots, yams, liver, fish, liver oils, egg yolks, butter, and cream.
Recommended dosage: 25,000 total units daily, taken in small amounts twice or three times a day.

B complexes important as a whole for energy production, to combat stress, hair and skin maintenance, digestive juice secretions, for blood vessels and eye maintenance. A breakdown of the B's follows:

Vitamin B_1 (thiamin) necessary for preventing fatigue and helps to change glucose into energy or fat. Wheat germ is the best source and rice polish is second best. It is found in cereal grains, dry beans, peas, nuts, kidneys, heart, soybeans, and lentils.
Recommended dosage: 50 mgs.

Vitamin B_2 (riboflavin) necessary for oxygen exchange in the soft tissues and the effective use of sugar and starch. A deficiency will cause mouth irritation, dermatitis, and an abnormal intolerance to light. It is found in liver, yeast, milk, spinach, lettuce and kale.
Recommended dosage: 50 mgs.

Vitamin B_3 (niacin) helps to eliminate mental depression and is an essential part of the enzyme system. It is found in liver, yeast, wheat germ, and kidney.
Recommended dosage: 50 mgs.

Vitamin B_6 necessary for the functioning of the central nervous system as well as protein, fat and sugar metabolism (you can see this is crucial for athletes in order to utilize protein). A deficiency will lead to loss of appetite, diarrhea, skin and mouth disorders and in the extreme, possible blindness. It is found in brewer's yeast, whole grains, milk, egg yolks, organ meat, cabbage, and beets. This vitamin seems to be greatly in vogue now.
Recommended dosage: 100 mgs.

Vitamin B$_{12}$	necessary for the functioning of the central nervous system, as well as protein, fat, and sugar metabolism. This is thought to be, by some, the most vital of the B's. A deficiency will lead to loss of appetite, decreased energy, diarrhea, skin and mouth disorder. It is found in brewer's yeast, liver, milk products, and lean meat. *Recommended dosage: 100 mgs.*
choline	a vitamin B complex that is important to fat metabolism and the proper functioning of the nervous system. It is found in liver, kidneys, egg holks, and whole grains. *Recommended dosage: 50 mgs.*
inositol	another antistress vitamin that is also important for hair growth, vision, your heart's action, and digestion. It is found in liver, yeast, wheat germ, whole wheat bread, oatmeal, unrefined molasses, and corn. *Recommended dosage: 50 mgs.*
pantothenic acid	a B complex vitamin that is necessary for keeping the adrenal glands working and combating stress. It is found in egg yolks, whole grains, cabbage, organ meats, and broccoli. *Recommended dosage: 50 mgs.*
folic acid (Vitamin B$_c$)	a B complex that is essential for growth. It is necessary for the proper division of body cells and the production of RNA and DNA; also needed for production of enzymes that assimilate amino acids and is used in conversion of sugar into energy. It is found in brewer's yeast, soy flour, and kidneys. *Recommended dosage: 30 mgs.*
biotin	a B complex vitamin that promotes growth. It is found in liver, kidneys, dried beans, cauliflower, chicken, whole eggs, hazel huts, mushrooms, peas, peanuts, and bacon. *Recommended dosage: 50 mgs.*
PABA	a B complex vitamin that is necessary for keeping color (some say it prevents graying) and helps to prevent sunburn. *Recommended dosage: 30 mgs.*

Vitamin B$_{15}$	(pangamic acid or calcium pangmate) not recognized as a vitamin by the FDA; it is treated as a food supplement. It is used by many Russian athletes and is *purported* to be effective in treating circulatory disorders, premature aging, and heart disease. It is found in whole grains, liver, brewer's yeast, and sunflower seeds. *Recommended dosage: 50 mgs.* (if you try it all, at your own risk)
Vitamin C	(ascorbic acid) one of the most important vitamins. It aids in the formation of collage, a substance that holds all cells together. It also builds up the resistance to shock and infection. A deficiency causes scurvy, bleeding gums, bruises, and the slow healing of wounds. Dr. Linus Pauling claims mega-doses of C help prevent colds. *Recommended dosage: 1,000 mgs.*
Vitamin D	necessary for growth of bones and teeth, prevents fatigue and helps burn sugar effectively. It is found in beef and chicken liver, fortified milk, egg yolks, butter, and fish oils. *Recommended dosage undetermined.*
Vitamin E	one of the most talked about and expounded, not because of its primary job, which is to supply oxygen to the cells, but because it is attributed to improve one's sexual prowess and to retard the aging process. It is stored mainly in the pituitary, adrenal, and sex glands. A deficiency leads to anemia. I highly recommend this for all adults in dosages of *400 IUs.*

Minerals

The many minerals in your body are interrelated in the synthesis of hemoglobin and the formation of red blood cells. They are crucial to nerve cell functions and body fluid maintenance; when you sweat, your body's minerals are coming out of your system. Humans require the following minerals: calcium, phosphorous, magnesium, sodium, potassium, sulfur, chlorine, iron, copper, cobalt, iodine, manganese, zinc, and fluorine. Because these minerals are found in most foods and a deficiency in them is not as likely as a vitamin deficiency, I will briefly describe them in this section but not chart them as completely as the vitamins.

Specifically, calcium is crucial for growth and the prevention of cramping. Dairy products, nuts, and milk are the best sources of calcium. Potassium, sodium, and chlorine are critical for the control and regulation of glandular secretions. Magnesium is involved in the nervous system and is found in brown rice, pecans, oatmeal, hazelnuts, walnuts, peanuts, Brazil nuts, corn, soya flour, barley, and whole wheat.

Your sweat is not just water. Based on this premise, several companies have drinks on the market that replace the minerals, or electrolytes, lost by perspiration. Some questions remain whether these drinks are of much use other than for quenching thirst or replacing lost fluids. The aforementioned minerals and the trace minerals zinc, cobalt, iron, iodine, and manganese can be found in protein-rich foods. I recommend a multi-mineral supplement each day to supply those which your diet might have missed. Of essential importance is potassium. A few years ago a number of people died from a potassium deficiency when they went on a liquid protein diet. If you go on a diet, include plenty of potassium from tomatoes, bananas or a potassium supplement.

Your Diet

As you get older your metabolism slows down, as does your testerone level. These developments, together with a reduced level of activity, result in unwanted inches. Our youthful, idyllic twenties are not so ideal when we realize the fact that weight gain is a reality. Have those extra beers or late-night pizzas begun to appear as an expanded waistline or as a double chin? Have you noticed that, even if you aren't eating any more than you did five or ten years ago, you are developing a paunch and your butt has grown? The average American gains one pound a year after the age of twenty-five; therefore, now is the time to establish good dietary habits.

Additionally, exercise is very important in conjunction with dieting, because it burns up calories. Some fat is lost when you diet without exercising, but other fat replaces the muscle. So remember, weight loss can occur without the jogging or sit-ups, but you will have higher body fat content, little muscle, and a less appealing personal appearance.

When more calories are burned than are taken in, weight is lost. This fact is the mainstay of the low-calorie diet that was so popular in weight reduction in the 1950s and 1960s. Each pound accounts for 3500 calories; each individual on the low-calorie diet maintains a daily calorie intake of 1000 to 2000 calories. Later, low-carbohydrate diets became the craze, popularized by the "Dr. Atkin's Diet Revolution." Seemingly, everyone on a diet was "counting carbs" and losing from ten to fourteen pounds in the first two weeks. A criticism of this low-carb diet is that the initial loss is caused by a loss of fluids. Because every gram of carbohydrate in the body can hold four grams of water, the body can't store as much water when carbs are greatly reduced and weight is lost. Another criticism of the low-carb diet is that it causes a significant energy loss because of the low blood-sugar level (carbohydrates are transformed into glucose, a simple sugar which gives you energy). Consequently, this reflects on your athletic performance and is conducive to irritability.

In the 1970s, the country was overcome with Dr. Herman Tarnower's "Scarsdale Medical Diet." Tarnower's diet attempts to offer rapid weight loss as well as balanced nutrition. Also, the Scarsdale Medical Diet, or SMD, allows for a lifetime weight-control program. This diet is generally referred to as a high-protein, low-calorie diet. There are no vitamin or mineral deficiencies. An intake of 1000 calories per day is averaged—broken up nutritionally into 43% protein, 22.5% fat, and 34.5% carbohydrates. Protein is supplied on the SMD in meat, fish, poultry, protein bread, and cheese; carbohydrates are cut back but included in fruits and vegetables and the protein bread. The SMD weight loss is significant because of the great limitation of fat consumption. When carbohydrates and fats are limited in intake and do not meet the body's caloric needs, the system draws upon stored fats that are already in the body in the form of excess weight. Ketones, partially metabolized products of the excess fat which the body burns off, are eliminated through the urine. Ketones also help curb one's appetite.

Dr. Tarnower states that, although his diet's combination of foods increases in fat metabolism and ketone production, they are not raised to an unhealthy level. He recommends the SMD for two weeks, followed by the "Keep-Trim Diet" which supposedly stabilizes the weight loss. If you want to lose more weight on this plan, you go on and off the SMD every two weeks until you obtain the desired weight.

Critics of this diet, myself included, say that the great reduction in carbohydrates will cause irritability and a loss of energy. Also, a significant amount of criticism considers the diet to be too high in protein. Your body can use only so much protein; the most efficient use of protein is as an energy source. I think eliminating dairy products from your diet deprives your body of a valuable source of protein, vitamins, and minerals. Additionally, Tarnower's "don't list" includes potatoes and rice. Potatoes, however, are valuable carbohydrates that also contain protein, vitamins, and minerals. Without butter or sour cream, they don't contain many calories. Rice, especially brown rice, is loaded with nutrients, and like potatoes (never fried or with oil) are a good source of energy. The SMD allows you all lean meats, yet ham and all pork products contain the highest fat and lowest protein count of any meat. Another comment: the SMD menu suggests lots of tuna fish, with the advice to wash the oil off. Wouldn't it be wiser to buy tuna packed in spring water?

Additionally, the SMD doesn't distinguish between the vegetables that are fattening, like lima beans and corn, and low-calorie ones, like broccoli and radishes. This same distinction is lacking in the fruits category: an apple is far more fattening than a grapefruit (although the SMD does always start off with half a grapefruit) or strawberries.

Nonetheless, Tarnower's diet books make very valid points and implement weight loss for numerous people. His variety of diets—the International, the Gourmet, the Money Saver and the Vegetarian—offer a wide and interesting choice.

For those of you that are healthy, with no restrictions from your doctor, I will first recommend simple weight-loss rules for you to follow. Then I will give you a very effective low-fat, low-calorie diet. The reason for the inclusion of the low-fat diet is because fats contain twice as many calories per gram as protein or carbohydrates: fats have nine calories per gram while carbs and protein have only four. As I stated earlier, although fats are essential to your diet, only 10 percent of your diet should consist of fats—or ten to twenty grams of fat per day. That's no low number. Even chicken breasts (without the skin), which I highly recommend, contain some fat.

LOW-FAT DIETING RULES

1. Limit yourself to no more than two light beers, two glasses of dry wine or two ounces of vodka mixed with grapefuit juice, cranberry juice or club soda. You may mix so you can have one light beer and one vodka daily. Avoid mixers such as tonic water, orange juice or Seven-Up.
2. Cut out all junk food—pastries, ice cream, cookies, cake, donuts, candy, etc.
3. Don't overeat! Second helpings are not necessary. Fortunately, you all don't have Italian or Jewish mothers pushing food at you until you have eaten everything on the table as well as in the refrigerator.
4. Avoid excess salt, dietetic foods, and drinks, because the sodium causes your body to retain excess water.
5. It is not impolite to refuse a dessert, especially a fattening one, at a dinner party.
6. Try having only one dinner of lean meat weekly. Eat broiled or baked fish at the rest of your dinners, with some meals of chicken without the skin. You can lose excess weight in surprising amounts by this diet change alone.

7. When having pasta, avoid serving with sauce. If necessary, use only a small portion of tomato sauce.
8. Never eat fried foods, especially chicken or potatoes.
9. Don't butter your bread. Never use it or sour cream on potatoes.
10. Don't use oil or conventional salad dressings on your salad. Try to use only vinegar or lemon juice on your salad. When necessary, use low-calorie dressings but avoid those with oil, sour cream, cheese or cream. Also avoid mayonnaise at all times.
11. Limit your fruits to low-calorie ones—grapefruit, strawberries, pine-apple, cantaloupe, honeydew melon, and cherries.
12. Limit yourself to lower calorie vegetables—broccoli, chick peas, string beans, eggplant, asparagus, cucumbers, lettuce, cabbage, celery, radishes, peppers, onions, mushrooms, spinach, tomatoes, and squash. Avoid fattening vegetables like corn, peas, lima beans, and carrots. If used, peas and carrots should consist of very small amounts.
13. Avoid all sauces on your food except those that are lemon-based or vinegar-based.
14. Eat slowly and chew your food carefully.
15. Try to eat a King's Breakfast, a Prince's Lunch and a Pauper's Dinner. It is better for your digestion. At your King's Breakfast, avoid any pork products, hash browns, french fries, pancakes, French toast or waffles.

DIETS FOR HEART PATIENTS

This is my variation of a daily food allotment given to heart patients. As you can see, it has 1000, 1400, 1600, 1800, and 2000 calorie diets.

Foods are divided into six groups called *exchange lists*. Portions of all foods within an exchange list have approximately equal carbohydrate and caloric values. By selecting different foods within each of the six exchange lists you can add variety to your meals. If, for example, you are to follow the 1600-calorie diet, your lunch would be: one choice (or serving) from each of the fruit, fat, and bread exchange lists, one serving from the vegetable A exchange list, two servings from the meat-exchange list (for example, two ounces of meat or one ounce of meat and one egg), and coffee or tea.

Important: It is important that you eat the amounts and kinds of food indicated in your Daily Food Allowance. The nutritive value of your meals and nourishments has been arranged to provide you with balanced nutrition throughout the day. *NOTE:* THE NUTRITIONAL ADEQUACY OF THE DIET IS DESTROYED IF THE PROTEIN SUPPLEMENTS ARE OMITTED.

Measuring food: Portion sizes must be accurate; weigh or measure when necessary. For this you will need a standard 8-oz. measuring cup and measuring spoons. All measurements are *level.* Cooked foods are measured *after* cooking. The use of a small scale to determine portion sizes is helpful until you are familiar with the appearance of the correct serving size.

Food preparation: Meats may be baked, boiled or broiled. Your foods may be prepared with the family meals, but be sure your portion is removed before any extra fat or flour is added. Fried foods should not be eaten. Combination dishes such as stews and casseroles may be eaten if permitted ingredients are used in the amounts specified in your Daily Food Allowance.

Avoid these foods: Sugar, candy, honey, jam, jelly, preserves, marmalade, syrup; pies, cakes, and cookies not listed in the bread exchange list; pastries, condensed milk, sweetened carbonated beverages, chewing gums containing sugar; fried, scalloped, and creamed foods; beer, wine, and other alcoholic beverages and snack items such as pretzels, popcorn, and potato chips.

Instructions: Follow the Daily Food Allowance for your specific calorie level, freely selecting from the food-group exchange lists. Follow exactly the portions as indicated for each meal. Do not omit any of the foods indicated in the Daily Food Allowance.

DAILY FOOD ALLOWANCE

	Number of servings for:				
Breakfast	1000 cal.	1400 cal.	1600 cal.	1800 cal.	2000 cal.
fruit	1	1	1	1	1
meat	1	1	1	1	1
bread	½	1	2	1	2
fat	–	1	2	2	2
coffee or tea (as desired)					
Lunch					
meat	2	2	2	2	3
vegetable list A	1	1	1	1	1
bread	–	1	1	1	1
fat	–	1	1	1	1
fruit	1	1	1	1	1
coffee or tea (as desired)					

Mid-afternoon   Protein drink with 8 oz. of skim milk

Dinner

meat	3	3	3	3	4
vegetable list A	1	1	1	1	1
vegetable list B	1	1	1	1	1
bread	–	1	1	1	1
fat	–	1	1	1	1
fruit	1	1	1	1	1
coffee or tea (as desired)					

Evening   Yogurt with wheat germ

   *or a milk-and-egg protein drink with 8 oz. of skim milk

VEGETABLE A EXCHANGE
Serving: raw—any amount
               cooked—1 cup

asparagus	lettuce
broccoli	mushrooms
brussels sprouts	okra
cabbage	peppers
cauliflower	radishes
celery	sauerkraut
cucumbers	spinach
eggplant	summer squash
green beans	tomatoes*
greens	wax beans

*Limit to one tomato or ½ cup
 tomato juice per serving

VEGETABLE B EXCHANGE
Serving: raw or cooked— ½ cup

beets	rutabagas
onions	turnips
pumpkin	winter squash

BREAD EXCHANGE

	Serving
bread	1 slice (no white bread)
biscuit	1
crackers, saltine	5
graham	2
round thin	6
muffin, plain	1
cereal, cooked	½ cup
dry (not pre-sweetened)	¾ cup
potatoes, white	½ cup
rice, preferably brown (cooked)	½ cup
spaghetti noodles (cooked)	½ cup
macaroni (cooked)	½ cup
egg noodles (cooked)	½ cup
corn	⅓ cup

MEAT EXCHANGE (Baked, boiled or broiled)

	Serving
meat (lean, no pork products), fish	1 oz.
luncheon meats	1 oz.
oysters, clams, shrimp	5 small
tuna, salmon (water pack)	¼ cup
egg	1

cheese	1 oz.	raspberries	1 cup
cottage cheese	¼ cup	strawberries	1 cup
peanut butter	1 tablespoon		

FAT EXCHANGE

Serving

butter or margarine	1 teaspoon
light cream	2 tablespoons
cream cheese	1 tablespoon
nuts	6 small
avocado	½" slice

FRUIT EXCHANGE (fresh, frozen or canned without sugar)

Serving

apricots	2 medium
apricot nectar	⅓ cup
banana	½ small
blackberries	1 cup
blueberries	⅔ cup
cantaloupe (6" diam)	¼ cup
cherries	10 large
dates	2
grapefruit	½ small
grapefruit juice	½ cup
grape juice	¼ cup
honeydew melon	1" slice
nectarine	1 medium
pineapple	½ cup
pineapple juice	⅓ cup
prunes, dried	2 medium
prune juice	¼ cup
raisins	2 tablespoons

ALLOWED AS DESIRED

Foods
  artificially sweetened beverages
  or soda pop containing less than
  10 calories per can, coffee or tea
  (no sugar or cream), fat-free
  broth or bouillon, rhubarb or
  cranberries (no sugar added),
  sour or dill pickles, unflavored
  gelatin

Seasonings
  herbs, spices, salt, mustard,
  lemon, flavor extracts, calorie-
  free sugar substitutes, vinegar

Supplements

Are you one of the conscientious few who eats three balanced meals a day? If so, you do not need supplements. However, most of us don't eat the balanced meals we should. We eat in restaurants or institutions where many of the vitamins and minerals are taken out of the food. Or we have not yet formed healthy eating habits since leaving our mothers' home cooking. Consequently, I recommend the vitamin and mineral supplements I noted earlier. When I was coaching at Notre Dame and in Denver with the Broncos, we regularly handed out protein supplements to our players, preferably a milk-and-egg protein supplement. If you are toning up without missing meals, then you probably don't need a protein supplement. If you must miss meals, however, and/or are more serious in your body building program, take two ounces of a good milk-and-egg protein supplement with eight ounces of papaya juice or skim milk daily.

BROC'S WEIGHT AND MUSCLE GAIN DIET

A. *Breakfast*
   1. 12 oz. of milk
   2. Fresh fruit (preferably melon, blueberries, strawberries, grapefruit or canteloupe)
   3. 2 slices of whole wheat bread
   4. 4–6 eggs, cheese or spinach omelette
   5. 6 oz. of breakfast meat, preferably steak (*NO BACON*)

B. *Mid-morning snack*
   1. Protein drink with 8 oz. of milk
   2. 1 banana
   3. Substitute for protein drink: 2 granola bars, peanuts, and milk

C. *Lunch* (Note: no milk at lunch)
   1. Salad—lettuce, tomatoes, carrots, radishes, onions
   2. 7 oz. of tuna fish, 10 oz of steak tartar (raw chuck ground with seasoning) or cheese and roast beef sandwich (½ lb.)
   3. 8–12 oz. of fruit juice
   4. Fresh fruit

D. *Mid-afternoon snack*
   1. Protein drink with pineapple or papaya
   2. Or a container of yogurt, with 2 tablespoons of wheat germ added

E. *Dinner*
   1. Salad (as much or more than lunch salad) with cee cee beans
   2. Shrimp, crab cocktail, 1 dozen clams, oysters, clam chowder or lobster bisque
   3. 12 oz. of steak, roast beef, liver or fish
   4. Spinach, broccoli or asparagus (1 cup)
   5. Peas or string beans (1 cup)
   6. Cauliflower or eggplant (1 cup)
   7. 2 slices of French, Italian, whole wheat, rye or pumpernickel bread
   8. Baked potato and skin (but no sour cream) or rice

F. *Night-time snack*
   1. 12 wheat thins or garlic rounds with sardines and anchovies or shrimp or crab cocktail
   2. Protein drink or yogurt with wheat germ or with brewer's yeast

G. *Foods to avoid:* Cakes, cookies, candy, pies, soda pop, dark liquor, white bread, sugar, lima beans, salad dressings (except for low cal.), pork products (especially bacon and hot dogs!)

H. *Best items for you:*
   1. Milk (at least a pint each day)
   2. Eggs (at least 2 daily)

I. *Don't Forget:* Pineapple and papaya are the best sources of digestive enzymes; your body can only utilize so much protein at one sitting, but by using the pineapple or papaya with the snacks you are better able to absorb the protein.

Steroids

A significant number of athletes and bodybuilders use steroids. Many of you have likely been exposed to the use of these drugs during your college sports programs. Despite their popularity in some circles, I am definitely opposed to steroids. Dangerous side effects caused by steroids are liver or kidney damage, impotency, skin problems and loss of hair. Aside from being unnatural, steroids cause you to "shrink" quickly after usage is stopped. Since steroids have not been used until recently, there has not been enough time for researchers to check for possible damages to human chromosomes. The children of those who took steroids might possibly be born with birth defects. I always recommend that my trainees avoid steroids as well as any other drugs. Similarly, your body deserves the same respect.

AEROBICS

Middle age and its notorious health concerns are not quite as far in the distance as they once were. Consequently, it is essential for you to focus now on weight maintenance and heart attack prevention. Aerobic exercising should play an integral role in this effort. Fortunately, aerobics can actually be fun, especially at this age when you have time and energy for activities such as swimming and bicycling.

Aerobic exercises stimulate both heart and lung activity long enough for beneficial changes to occur in the body. These exercises involve the maximum intake and utilization of air and result in an increased aerobic capacity. ("Aer" is the Greek word for air.) The respiratory muscles increase in endurance, and the heart becomes a more effective pump. Consequently, there is a greater intake and diffusion of oxygen to the blood. The increased aerobic capacity leads to greater endurance – an equivalent to physical fitness. Physical fitness is an important part of good health, so the relationship between aerobic capacity and feeling good is simple and direct. Aerobic exercising has also been effective in combating injuries to the body and producing a higher level of mental alertness.

The goals of aerobic exercising are to increase performance and endurance and to adapt the body's support organs (bones, muscles, joints, and others) to accommodate the increased physical activity. Exercises designed to improve aerobic capacity must be of a dynamic nature, involving at least one-sixth of all the body's muscles. The only way to improve or maintain one's endurance is to train. Training is measured doses of overexertion. The heart must be placed under long-term, sustained physical activity.

Interestingly, the first thirty to sixty seconds of exertion are anaerobic, or without oxygen; the body does not need oxygen to reach the muscles for a response. However, when this anaerobic response is over, the muscles need oxygen to perform. Most weight training is anaerobic. Circuit training, on the other hand, can be aerobic.

Although, at your age, you may not be greatly susceptible to heart disease. I think that it is a good idea to read the following to forewarn you about such problems. Additionally, as I have been stressing throughout the book, the present is an opportune time in your life to set patterns for health.

The cardiovascular system consists of the heart and lungs. The heart pumps blood, which carries oxygen to all body parts. As we exercise more, we increase the need for oxygen to be delivered to our muscles. Training will increase the heart's efficiency, strengthening it, and thereby increase its pumping capacity.

As one in three adults suffer from a major or minor cardiac circulatory ailment, I strongly recommend an aerobic conditioning program. It is ideal for preventive measures in conditioning the body against a heart attack, and can also have a restorative effect on an impaired circulation.

As your respiratory muscles strengthen, they reduce their resistance to air flow, allowing greater amounts of air into the lungs; the more oxygen you take in, the more the blood is pumped. A strengthened heart pumps more blood with each beat, reducing the number of strokes per minute. An increased aerobic capacity causes the heart to strain less, in turn reducing blood pressure and the amount of work the heart has to do. Muscle tone is also increased with a greater aerobic endurance, allowing better circulation. Finally, aerobic conditioning increases the amount of red blood cells and hemoglobin (the part of the blood that carries oxygen), making the blood a more efficient oxygen carrier.

I recommend a complete physical examination and electrocardiogram (ECG) before undertaking an aerobic exercise program. The ECG should be taken while you are exercising, such as on a treadmill or a stationary bicycle. Such tests should determine any existing health or heart problems that would cause an appropriate adjustment in your program. Approach aerobic conditioning less vigorously and proceed at a slower rate if you have been inactive for a few years. Such conditions as obesity, diabetes or heart problems may prohibit exercises such as running or jogging, but it is possible to achieve aerobic conditioning through another less strenuous exercise, such as walking.

The benefits of each exercise depend on the duration and intensity involved. The minimum program for fitness is three thirty-minute exercises per week. Therefore, if you jog five miles per hour (mph), you must walk twice as long to burn the same amount of calories and to earn the same aerobic value. If you cycle at ten mph, you burn the same amount of calories as jogging at five mph. Calculate your pulse rate (the number of heart beats per minute) to see if the physical activity is sufficient to produce the desired training effect. Do this by placing your thumb on the right or left side of your neck. Then keep time with a watch with a second-hand and count your heart beats for ten seconds. The intensity of the exercise should raise the pulse by 60%. The minimum heart rate for a training effect should be your age subtracted from 170. Remember to ascertain the exercise's intensity only a few moments after completion of the exercise. The heart rate should not exceed your age subtracted from 220, or you have overtaxed your heart and must proceed more slowly.

In his book *The New Aerobics,* Dr. Kenneth H. Cooper uses a point system in addition to the increased pulse rate to determine the effectiveness of each exercise. The more energy expended with each exercise, the more points received. Following Cooper's point-chart program, the exercises become progressively more intense, though not necessarily in amount but in the intensity in which they are performed. For example, if you are on a 2-mile running program three times a week, the distance would not have to change, but your time should decrease with each succeeding week to achieve the benefits of aerobic conditioning. More points are allotted in accordance with the intensity of the exercise, with the goal being thirty points per week—Cooper's minimum standard of fitness.

My criticism of Cooper's point system is that equal points are not awarded for energy expended, being somewhat low for some athletic activities such as lacrosse or rugby. Also, it should be recognized that twenty minutes of effort is not four times as effective as five minutes, nor are four sessions per week as effective as two.

In summary, aerobic conditioning is highly beneficial. You achieve a healthier cardiovascular system; tension is reduced; you feel more invigorated and alert. Some diabetics on the program have found that the exercises improve the body's capability to process sugar, which reduces insulin intake. Remember not to strain yourself to the point of exhaustion in the beginning. This will defeat the program's purpose and leave you fatigued. You should exercise regularly to build up your aerobic capacity. Exercising at the same time daily can help you, as does exercising with a group.

Circuit Weight Training

Are you interested in receiving good cardiovascular conditioning as you weight train? If so, I recommend circuit weight training. Multistations of weight-training equipment, such as Nautilus, Universal, Paramount or freeweight stations (or some other combination of equipment) are involved in this type of training. Though not nearly as good a conditioner as running, swimming or bicycling, circuit training works that heart and blood vessels of yours, along with developing and toning your body.

However, when I was coaching full time, I only employed circuit training for maintenance programs and for the logistics advantages: several individuals can be pushed through the program in a short amount of time. I usually don't recommend circuit training for bodybuilding because I believe you gain more from the exercises when they are done together by body part—for example, completing your bench presses together before continuing with your chin-ups or military presses. Better development of each body part is best achieved this way.

In the usual Nautilus circuit, you start with the largest muscle groups first, as you work on the hip and back machine, then either the leg extension, leg curl and leg press or the combination leg extension-leg press machine; then the chest machine, which combines a seated upright bench press with an incline fly to work all parts of your chest. Resting only thirty seconds between each part of the compound machines, you then proceed to either the Nautilus lat pulldown or combination back machine, which has a pullover machine and a frontal lat pulldown. Next, you move to the double shoulder machine, which works all heads of your deltoids (or the trap machine first, if your club has it). You proceed to the double-arm machine which consists of the curling machine for your biceps, and tricep extension for triceps or the back of your arms. Nautilus recommends one set of twelve reps to failure on each machine. They also advise you to use smooth motions and to slowly return to the starting position. This return to the starting position allows you to utilize the negative aspect of the exercise. Remember, the positive aspect occurs when you lift the weight and the negative aspect occurs when you let the weight down. Both movements play important roles in exercise.

In the Universal circuit, you usually start with the leg extension for eight to twelve reps follows. Yet, be careful with the leg press: don't do full extensions on the leg press if you have any knee problems. The next station is the sit-up board, followed by the bench press, the chin-up bars, the military press, the low pulley for curls or cable rowing, and lastly, the lat pulldown.

If you use the Universal or Paramount circuit, rest thirty seconds between stations. When you start, go through the station for one set in the first week, then two sets in the second week for three workouts. In the third week, try three sets of each circuit three times a week. This schedule should tone you up and help to condition you. One advantage of the Paramount equipment is its dual stacks with which each arm, as well as each leg, can be worked independently. Therefore, if one of your arms or legs is stronger than the other, you will become equally developed; the stronger limb won't take up the slack.

However, you can set up a circuit with free weights for a combination of free weights and machines, as I did at Notre Dame. The aforementioned equipment is not necessary, as I noted earlier. A typical circuit like this would include a quad-ham machine, followed by a squat rack, preferably a power rack with pins (which is safer than two bare racks), a bench press, an incline press, a chin-up bar or lat pull-down, a rack with a bar or dumbbells for curls, and a bench with another E-Z curl bar for lying tricep extensions for the back of your arms. You could try a sit-up board first, then a Roman chair last, either before or after use of this equipment.

Despite the type of circuit you use, make sure you initially stretch out and warm up before you begin. Don't take more than thirty seconds between each set or you will lose the aerobic benefits of circuit training.

Running

Many of you may shudder at the thought of running because of the demanding role it played in your school sports practices. Yet running (or jogging) is one of the most effective aerobic exercises. Strength and muscle tone increase; your blood circulation improves. The most visible benefit of running is the weight loss. Walking at one mph burns off 135 calories per hour, and walking at four mph can burn off 400 calories. Jogging at five mph uses up 550 calories, at five and one-half mph, 630 calories, and at seven mph, 750 calories. Running also suppresses the appetite: blood is taken away from the stomach and used on those muscles involved in running. However, it is possible that a rapid weight loss may be a result of overexertion. Additionally, running is an exercise that is not greatly affected by the weather and does not require a great deal of time. Outside of buying a few articles of running wear, the costs are also relatively small.

Not only does running utilize a large number of calories, it acts as a safeguard against heart attack with its significant cardiovascular benefits. The number of red blood cells increases, breathing becomes deeper, and the hemoglobin in the blood become more acidic, making the red blood cells attract oxygen more readily. As the lungs gain in their oxygen consumption, the heart strengthens and in turn reduces the blood pressure.

Also, running reportedly promotes mental health by combating depression, reducing anxiety, and changing self-destructive patterns such as drinking and smoking. Theoretically, as your body strengthens, so does your mind. As the body becomes more conditioned and attractive, one's self-image will most likely improve. Insomnia has also been treated successfully with a running program. The increased exercise produces a healthy fatigue and you sleep more deeply.

Your form while running is important. As you run, the first part of the foot to touch the ground should be your heel—coming down as softly as possible. Avoid pounding the ground. The legs should fully extend with each stride and the faster the pace, the longer the stride. The arms should be flexible and the hands should not raise up much higher than the waist. Run with our fists lightly closed, not clenched; keep your eyes up, shoulders relaxed and avoid leaning forward too much. Your posture should be as comfortable as possible. Lastly, remember to establish a rhythm to your breathing to help you set your pace.

Wearing the proper equipment is essential to a running program. Inappropriate clothing can increase the likelihood of an accident. A good, well-fitting shoe is the runner's most important piece of equipment. Shoes cannot only enhance performance, they guard against injury to the knee, legs, hips, and joints. The running shoe's purpose is to protect the foot from the constant pounding on the pavement. A properly fitted shoe should fit firmly on the foot, but not too tightly, with about a half inch between the big toe and the front of the shoe. Because the foot swells while running, it is advisable to buy a half size bigger than you normally wear. There should also be a wedge on the shoe back that lifts the heel up, relieving the strain on the Achilles tendon and calf muscles. The shoe should be flexible enough to allow comfortable movement and should have a flat heel and an innersole for solid support. The sole should be made of a thick, rubberized material: ripple-type soles are best for pavement jogging; gripper-type soles work best on a cinder track or dirt path. Sock wear is optional, though they are helpful in preventing blisters. Your shirts and shorts should be made of a porous material to allow the body to breathe and absorb perspiration. Clothing should also be lightweight and comfortable. Cotton is ideal but nylon should be avoided as it contains too much of the body heat. The human body adapts well to environmental conditions if given the chance. Allow a week for the body to adjust to changes in the weather or a higher altitude. The clothing you wear can help your body adjust more readily. In extreme heat, you can run shirtless, and in the cold weather a hat (and gloves) prevents one-half of your body heat from escaping through the scalp.

Many courses are available for a running program. Grassy paths in a park are ideal because of their soft resiliency. But they are often scarce and may be dangerous for night running because your limited vision may not see holes and bumps. A dirt path is also ideal if it isn't covered with stones. Avoid too soft courses, such as sand, as they can overstress the feet and legs and lead to hyperextension of the joints. Most cinder and wood tracks are circular, and joggers find them to be boring and repetitive. Asphalt or concrete roads are the most accessible to runners. Though they are usually smooth, minor aches and pains may arise from the constant pounding. Adjusting your form may correct this. Changing the course or path you run on helps prevent boredom. Try to avoid running near traffic or factories. The carbon monoxide given off inhibits the body's capacity to carry oxygen and may cause dizziness and shortness of breath.

It is important to replace lost body fluids from the increased perspiration and salt loss. Fluids should be taken slowly, and using salt tablets or more table salt on your food will compensate for the salt deficit. Allow two to three hours after eating before you run and make the pre-run meal light. In fact, it is preferable to run on an empty stomach. With a full stomach, the blood you need to supply oxygen to the muscles is in the stomach aiding in digestion. Consequently, you tire more easily without the blood and oxygen you need to fuel your muscles. Also, refrain from smoking thirty minutes before and after any such strenuous exercise. The carbon monoxide inhaled cuts down on the hemoglobin's ability to carry oxygen. Many joggers have found running to be an impetus to quit smoking.

Runners are susceptible to a variety of injuries. Preventive measures include proper warm-up and warm-down exercises, the correct running form, and the right equipment. Your warm-up and warm-down exercises should include sit-ups, as running does not do much for the stomach. Also, various calisthenics are helpful in limbering up the body before a run and warming it down afterwards. Toe touching, side stretches, and leg extensions all increase the flexibility necessary for a safe and productive run. To strengthen the calf muscles, stand with your feet parallel, toes pointed slightly inward. Raise up on your left leg, shifting your total body weight to that leg. Alternate with your right leg. Here is another exercise for stretching the calves: stand straight, about three feet from a wall. Lean forward with your palms extended into the wall, keeping your feet as flat as possible on the ground. To strengthen the ankles, hop lightly on both feet. The knees can be strengthened by dropping from a standing position, bending into a deep squat (see the flexibility chapter for more stretches).

Certain problems may be caused by improper equipment. "Runner's toe" is a hemorrhage under the toenail caused by jamming the toes against the front of the shoe. Though not serious, it is a sign that you need a better-fitting shoe. Blisters may be caused by too much friction between the skin and shoe. Powdering the foot with talcum powder and wearing a cotton sock can help relieve this problem. If you get a blister, lance it with a sterilized needle, apply first-aid dressing, and bandage it, making sure the area is kept clean to prevent infection. Arch pains may arise from problems such as improper shoes or a bone defect. A foot-care specialist—a podiatrist—may be able to fit you with a special device to correct running problems and, in extreme cases, perform corrective surgery. Hip injuries can be caused by unequal leg lengths. A lift placed in the shorter leg's shoe by a podiatrist can correct this.

Overtaxing of unconditioned muscles and ligaments can result in painful injuries. Knees may become swollen with liquid because of overuse. An exercise to alleviate or prevent this is to sit on the edge of a desk and raise your leg until it is fully extended in front of you, lowering it slowly. This strengthens the quadriceps, which are the muscles in front of the thigh. Shin splints are a pain in the front portion of the lower leg and may be caused by pounding the pavement too hard. Chronic overuse of a muscle can lead to tendonitis, which is a pain and swelling of the affected area. Again, this may arise from improper footwear or lack of a warm-up and warm-down period. Resting will help alleviate the pain from tendonitis. Return to running gradually. Sprains may result from a severe fall or twisting of a muscle. Ice will help to limit the swelling. However, you should not resume running until you can walk painlessly. Taking one tablet of vitamin C for every hour you run is effective in protecting the muscles and ligaments against injury. Remember to allow yourself time to condition your muscles. Overtaxing yourself can lead to serious injury and set back any aerobic benefits you may have gained. I discourage people from starting directly on a running program unless they have been exercising regularly. Walking allows the heart to accommodate the new physical demands and also allows the body's muscles and tendons to adjust as well. With a doctor's approval, a jogging program may be undertaken if the aerobic conditioning received from walking is sufficient. Remember to work slowly into a program if you have remained inactive for some years.

Swimmers

With their superior muscles and well-developed cardiovascular systems, swimmers probably have the healthiest and best-toned bodies among athletes. As an aerobic program, swimming not only offers such possible developments, but it necessitates only a relatively small investment of time and can be enjoyed almost anywhere, anytime.

Swimming's dynamic movement exercises all the major muscle groups and is very good for the back and spine. I highly recommend swimming for those who cannot use an aerobic running program; swimming is as efficient as running for the cardiovascular system. One mile of swimming equals four miles of jogging in the benefits and conditioning they produce. Calorie-wise, a breaststroke will use up 450 calories per hour; the backstroke burns up 450 calories and the crawl will use up 800 calories per hour. An aerobic swimming program should last for at least ten minutes per swim so as to produce the desired benefits.

Swimming increases the lung's capacity for holding oxygen. The added water pressure placed on the body strengthens the oxygen intake process, which helps the lungs work more efficiently. The capillaries—extensions of the arteries that carry the blood from the heart—increase in number.

The capillaries are at the site of oxygen pickup from the lungs and of oxygen transfer to the muscle cells in the blood. As the number of capillaries increase, the higher and quicker the oxygen can get to the muscles involved.

Swimming is also not just another summer sport. Most apartment complexes, municipal recreation centers, and YMCAs offer swimming facilities. Heated pools help combat prevailing weather conditions; I strongly urge use of them. The body does not have to adjust to varying temperatures, and there is less risk of accidents. Swimming, in fact, offers fewer chances of strain or injury than almost any other sport.

When swimming, the body should be horizontal with the head held low. This gives the least resistance to swimming. Arms should enter and pull the water with straight elbows. Once in the water, bend your arms to a 90-degree angle, returning to an extended position before coming up out of the water. Hold the hands outwards diagonally as they enter the water, as this cuts down on water resistance and propels you forward efficiently. For your breathing, you should inhale air when you start to bring your arm out of the water. Breathe in with your nose and exhale through both nose and mouth.

When buying a suit, choose a snug-fitting suit made of a lightweight, flexible material. Loose suits increase resistance to movement in water and impair your buoyancy. Heavy suits, such as cutoffs, will weigh you down. Since it is not only lightweight but it stands up well to chlorine and salt water, nylon is ideal. Washing your suit after a swim helps to avoid discoloration.

Showering after a swim with a good moisturizing soap will restore your body's natural oils. Skin and eye problems may result from high chemical levels in a pool. An allergic reaction from swimming in fresh water (that contains parasites), "swimmer's itch," can be relieved with the use of calamine lotion. "Swimmer's ear" is an irritation of the ear canal from a bacterial infection. It is good habit to dry your ears with rubbing alcohol after a swim. Earplugs also prevent infections. Goggles help prevent chlorine irritation in the eyes.

Cramps occur while swimming from a muscle tightening due to a lack of blood. Most pass momentarily and can be relieved by applying pressure firmly. Sprains occur from overtaxing weak muscles and training insufficiently. "Swimmer's shoulder" is the overuse of the overhand swing. Flexibility exercises and proper warm-up and warm-down procedures can help you avoid these muscular problems. Jumping jacks, shoulder rolls, leg stretches, and torso twists all help strengthen the muscles before a swim in addition to supplying flexibility. To warm up before a swim, lie flat in the water, face down. Holding onto the edge of the pool, kick your feet back and forth. At the same time, turning your head sideways to breathe in and out in rhythm to your kicking.

If you choose to swim in fresh or sea water, there are some extra precautions you should take. Do not swim when no others are present, especially when there is no lifeguard. Do not swim immediately after a heavy meal, as the muscle cramps you may get could impair your swimming ability (remember this at a pool, too). Although a swim in the ocean can be invigorating, watch out for dangers such as jellyfish, sharks, changing currents and tides, and undertows. Do not take risks.

One last note: any doctor will tell you that swimming is about the best existing therapy for recuperating from a knee injury.

Bicycling

Probably one-half of the guys in America use a bicycle—not simply for transportation purposes but for exercise and enjoyment. As an aerobic exercise, bicycling is highly recommended because, like running and swimming, it produces great overall endurance through its continual, dynamic stimulation of both lung and heart activities. Additionally, cycling burns up a significant number of calories: 270 calories are used up at six miles per hour; at ten mph, 400 calories are used in an hour. The buttocks, quadriceps, and calves are the muscles that are strengthened. Yet, the muscles that are involved in cycling tire sooner than the heart, giving the cyclist an advantage of never having to be concerned with problems of overexertion.

Stationary bicycles offer excellent testing or conditioning opportunities also. Yet they have all the advantages and none of the disadvantages of outdoor riding. An attached ergometer can help determine your exercise tolerance, which is helpful in undertaking an aerobic program on a bicycle. If you choose or are restricted to a stationary bicycle, select one with as large a flywheel as possible. Many come with speed and mileage indicators—good aids for charting your progress. Also, make sure your bike has brake resistance. These types of bicycles are recommended for knee injuries, too.

It is quite easy to keep track of your aerobic progress on a cycling exercise program. Simply add a tachometer feature, which determines revolutions per minute, to your bike and have a stopwatch at hand. First, record your pulse rate. Starting out on your ride, proceed slowly until you reach your training pulse rate (remember, the ideal rate is 170 minus your age). After five minutes, ride at your full speed for five to ten minutes. Your goal should be sixty to eighty rpm's pedaling. Decrease your speed gradually to wind down your ride with a five-minute warm-down. This program should be repeated four times weekly, increasing your time spent at full speed gradually. As your conditioning improves, you will find you need to increase the intensity of your exercise to maintain your training pulse rate.

When buying a bike, choose a model with a light frame and large wheels. I do not suggest folding bikes. Changeable gears increase the intensity of the exercise because of the shifting speeds. In addition to a tachometer, a stopwatch is helpful for calculations of speed and duration. The seat should be positioned so that the leg is fully extended to reach the pedal. When riding, the ball of the foot, not the toes or arch, should be placed on the pedal. When pedaling, pedal completely around, not allowing one foot to rest as the other leg pumps.

As with most activities, the proper conditioning and appropriate equipment reduces the likelihood of injuries. Customizing a bike leads to structural problems, as does poor maintenance. For night riding, you should have reflectors and headlight attachments on your bike, in addition to wearing reflectorized clothing. Helmets should be worn, since statistics show head injuries account for most fatal cycling injuries. Bike paths should be utilized whenever possible. However, because cyclists usually share the roadways with cars, trucks, and motorcycles, they must be alert while riding through traffic. Most cycle-car accidents are caused by the carelessness of the biker, however.

In the event of a cycling accident, remember the first-aid guidelines: immobilization, compression, and elevation, or I.C.E.

Racquetball

Racquetball is the youngest of the racquet sports, and probably a sport to which you were introduced in school and enjoyed immensely. If played at a full pace, racquetball offers great aerobic benefits. On the court, short bursts of activity are followed by brief periods of inactivity. Consequently, a high level of aerobic fitness is actually needed for the endurance involved in an intense game.

A competitive game in which racquets are used to serve and return the ball, racquetball can be played by two, three or four players. To serve the ball, a player bounces it on the floor and strikes it so that it hits the front wall and rebounds behind the short line on the court floor. The object is to serve or return the ball such that your opponent cannot return the ball without bouncing it twice on the floor. A game is won with the scoring of twenty-one points.

A standard racquetball court has four walls, a 20-foot wide, 20-foot high, and 40-foot long playing area that is divided equally into a front and back court, which is separated by a short line. The grips involved in the game are the forehand and the backhand. The racquet should be gripped such that the "V" formed by the thumb and forefinger is directly on top of the handle.

In addition to a racquet, ball, and partner(s), additional equipment

should be purchased for the game. Buy a good pair of gym shoes that
have a nonslip sole. Wear socks so as to avoid blistering. As with tennis,
the clothing should allow freedom of movement without being too baggy.
Wristbands and sweatbands absorb the perspiration. If you find that a
wristband does not sufficiently absorb and your grip becomes affected, try
wearing racquetball gloves.

Eye injury is a real possibility because of the confined playing space
and the high speeds at which the ball travels. Eyeguards or goggles can be
worn for injury prevention. During game time, keep out of your partner's
way and know where the ball is at all times. Like other sports, proper
alertness will contribute to avoidance of accidents, just as will proper
conditioning. Limber up before a game with knee bends and torso
stretches. This will help with the strain that racquetball places on the
body's back and knees, which is caused by the common half-crouch
position with half-flexed knees and extended lower back. Achilles
tendonitis occurs with overuse of an unconditioned muscle, and can be
relieved by resting the affected area. Sprains, pulls, and inflammations all
arise from an overstress or improper technique. Again, remember to
warm up and warm down properly with exercises such as jumping jacks,
toe touches and side stretches to increase your flexibility.

Lastly, over 2,000 racquetball clubs exist nationwide. Choose your
club by following guidelines similar to those included in this book.

Tennis

Like racquetball, tennis is another enjoyable exercise that can have
aerobic benefits when played at an intense, full pace. Don't let the fact
that you weren't a college star on the courts deter you from taking up
tennis again. The benefits received aerobically are many, because of the
very dynamic movements in tennis. The cardiovascular system is placed
under great stress to meet the extra muscle demands on your shoulders,
forearms (playing arm only), thighs, and calves. This stress also
strengthens these muscles. The calories usage in tennis can be a very
effective weight control. A game of doubles uses up about 300 calories per
hour, while singles play will burn off 450 calories per hour.

Many skills go into a successful game of tennis. Accuracy is a major
factor in placement of the ball; anticipation is important in receiving your
opponent's ball. Putting the ball where you want it to go can be practiced
against a backboard.

Joining a club is another way of game improvement (see my chapter
on choosing a club). Investigate the club thoroughly, but most
importantly, look into individual and group instruction, class size,
instruction time, court charges, and the like. In choosing a teacher, make

certain his or her personality and teaching style are agreeable to you. A teacher should help you learn (or relearn) the basics of tennis, as well as improving your skills.

Tennis "pro shops" usually offer the best merchandise at the most value and have a knowledgeable staff to assist in your choice of equipment. Rackets are available in wood, metal, fiberglass, and composite materials. Choose a racket suitable to your style and technique. Choose a well-gripped racket that is not too heavy and will not weigh you down as you play. Stringing the racket also should be suited to your individual needs. A racket can be strung with light-to-heavy tension. The average player should have his racquet strung at fifty-four to fifty-six pounds per square inch of tension. Strings can be made of a natural catgut material or of a nylon, manmade fiber.

Balls are uniformly pressured balls and tend to leak pressure with use. Tennis is played on a variety of court surfaces: grass court, for fast play; clay court, for slower play. Concrete and astroturf surfaces are also used.

Your shoes should be chosen according to the court surface. You need a gripping sole for a grass or clay court to prevent sliding. For concrete and synthetic courts, rugged-faced soles with good support are needed. Clothing should allow freedom of movement and should be lightweight. Light cottonwear is best. In choosing clothes for your game, don't sacrifice comfort for design. Socks reduce chafing; headbands and wrist sweatbands absorb perspiration. It is a good idea to check with a club first if there is a question on the old rule of wearing only whites.

Flexibility, proper warm-up and warm-down exercises, conditioning, and proper technique help to prevent injuries. Tennis requires flexibility in the torso and upper body. The knees and arms are also used extensively. A player's flexibility is improved by such stretching exercises as sit-ups, knee bends, toe touches, arm extensions, neck twists and leg stretches. Dumbbell curls (promoting and supporting) with the arms, and leg raises, help to strengthen muscles used in a tennis game. Strengthening the abdomen, buttocks, and thigh muscles takes much strain off the back. Short-distance running and agility drills, such as running sideways form one side of the court to the other, are good training exercises. Slowly stretching body parts gradually lengthens the ligaments and muscle/ tendon units.

Injuries incurred during a game of tennis can be worked on. Shoulder injuries that result from the straining of the shoulder joints can be relieved by proper warm-ups and flexibility exercises, in addition to light weight-training exercises. Overstretching and overwork of the muscles and tendons in the arm and elbow result in "tennis elbow" or tendonitis, which can be prevented by proper weight training and a correction in playing technique. "Tennis knee" is an irritation of the cartilage of the knee joint that deep-knee bends can help you avoid. "Tennis leg" is a tear of the calf muscle on the inner side of the leg. This is usually caused by the player's turning to strike a sudden backhand. Resting the leg until you can walk painlessly is the best treatment.

There are many other activities that can involve aerobic conditioning. Mountain climbing, hiking, rowing, paddling, brisk walking and conditioning calisthenics are all good exercises that increase your aerobic conditioning and endurance. Use common sense in your choice of activity. Overtaxing and straining yourself will only lead to fatigue and defeat the purpose of an aerobic program. Straining yourself without the proper conditioning in any sport or activity can also create more damage than good. Remember that most injuries and accidents can be avoided with the proper equipment and appropriate warm-up and warm-down exercises and strengthening exercises particular to the activity. I recommend swimming and bicycling for those who are prohibited from running or a more strenuous sport because of health or heart problems. In conclusion, a general rule in any aerobic exercise is to remember that the intensity must be increased gradually for you to benefit from aerobic endurance.

FLEXIBILITY

Stretching increases your body's degree of flexibility. Your lack of stretching will reduce your ability to move into positions that were previously possible, especially in youth. Fortunately, stretching has become more popular recently, partially because of the focus by the media on different aspects of sports, including the various training regimens. Numerous books are available on stretching, along with innumerable articles in sports magazines and newspapers. This chapter will supply you with the basic stretching exercises to improve your flexibility, but it is not a complete listing of all the existing stretches. If you want to research stretching exercises further, you will find that there are literally hundreds of stretches.

Flexibility is important to those of you involved in weight-training routines. When you lift weights you are contracting your muscles. If your muscles are pre-stretched before contraction, more fibers in the muscles will be utilized when needed under a heavy load. A muscle contraction is not as strong as it could be when contracted from a relaxed starting position. To gain the most from your aerobic activities as well as from your weight training, you need to stretch for three to six minutes before your workout, game or run, and three to six minutes after. Both your warm-up and your cool-down should include a stretching period. Stretching is especially crucial before your leg routine and before any running. If you are not stretched out, you could possibly strain a muscle or get what is commonly called a hamstring pull.

Thus, there are many significant benefits from stretching: maintenance of body mobility, injury prevention, and training-room improvements; a good stretching program is highly profitable. I recommend that you do any one or two exercises per body part each day. Also, don't limit yourself to stretching only during a workout or before a run or game. You can stretch daily in your home. Remember to begin slowly and to refrain from jerking and holding the stretched position for more than the necessary few seconds.

The need for stretching in all animals, including us, is demonstrated by the stretching done regularly by your dog. Watch him stretch out when he wakes up. Don't you feel better when you stretch your arms in the morning upon awakening? Increase your body flexibility and feel better at the same time—select the exercises you want to do and begin today. If you have time for sports or weight lifting, you have time to stretch.

A1: Circular Shoulder Rotation
Rotate the neck in a full circle, extending the head as far back as it will go. Use the same motion for the arms and trunk, completing at least 10 full circles. These exercises will loosen up the key muscle groups.

B1-2: Hamstring Trunk Rotation
This should be done with both legs straight and your hands on the ground. Attempt to touch your right foot to the left hand and the left foot to the right hand. Stretch the hamstrings 2 to 3 times in this manner.

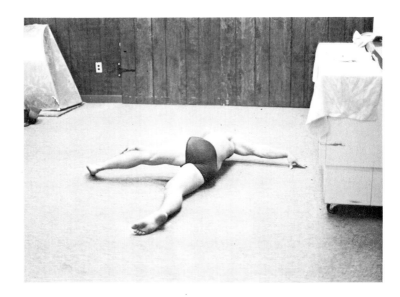

C1-3: Hamstring Stretch I (left)
This exercise will loosen up the
hamstring muscle, which
together with the quadricep
provides 80 percent of the knee's
support. With hands fully
extended into the air, bend over,
being careful not to bend your
knees. The motion should be a
smooth movement. Be careful
not to jerk down and pull the
hamstrings. Grasp your ankles
and continue the motion until
your head touches your knees.

D1-2: Hamstring Stretch II
Start in a position such as the
one used in the circular shoulder
rotation but this time spread the
legs as far apart as possible.
Grasp the ankle with both hands
and attempt to touch your chin
to your knee. Repeat with both
legs 2 to 3 times.

E1-2: Partner Stretch
With your partner facing you, stretch open the legs until your feet touch the inside of his ankles. While grasping each other's wrists, pull back while your partner offers resistance. Repeat the exercise with reversed roles.

F1: Flip-Over Hamstring Stretch
Lying flat on the ground with your hands at your side, lock the knees and spread your legs as far apart as possible. Raise your legs until your toes touch the ground. Those suffering from lower-back problems should avoid this exercise.

G1-2: Bent-Over Hamstring Stretch
Starting in the spread-eagle position, place your hands behind your head or straight out and attempt to touch the ground with your head. Stretch slowly and avoid jerking.

H1: Hamstring Groin Stretch I
Place your leg at a right-angle position and grasp the ankle of the horizontal leg while attempting to touch your chin to your knee.

I1: Hamstring Groin Stretch II
Starting in the same position as
the previous exercise, grasp the
ankle of the standing leg and
touch the chin to the knee while
keeping your knees straight.

J1–2: Lotus Groin Stretch
Position yourself with ankles
meeting on your hands and
knees. Push down on the knees
and try to touch them to the
ground.

K1: Hamstring Lower-Back Stretch *(left, top)*
Beginning in a sitting position, grasp behind the calf and try to touch your forehead to your knees. Be careful not to bounce down; rather, do it in one easy motion to maximize the benefit to the hamstring and lower back.

M1: Hurdler's Stretch *(below)*
Change your position slightly from the previous exercise by bending one knee while keeping the legs apart at a right angle. Stretch the hamstrings by leaning forward on your straight leg while you try to keep the knee touching the ground to stretch the quadriceps.

L1: Modified Hurdler's Stretch
With both legs spread apart, keep the knee touching the ground and then attempt to touch your forehead to your knee.

N1–2: Negative Dip

This is the finest stretching
exercise for upper-body
flexibility. Just raise yourself up
on the dipping bar and then let
yourself down slowly, doing the
negative aspect of the dip only.

O1–3: Leg Extension
Extend your leg in all possible
positions, keeping the knee stiff.
You may need some help from a
partner to get the full extension.

P1-2: Bar Stretch
Hold a bar at the ends in front
of you at shoulder height.
Extend the bar slowly over your
head and down to waist level.

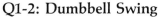

Q1-2: Dumbbell Swing

This is actually a great warm-up exercise that affects about every muscle group in the body. Start with a very light weight, so you won't strain yourself. Stand comfortably with your feet about 18 to 24 inches apart. Hold the dumbbell with a hand-over-hand safe grip and, in a crouched squat, start with the dumbbell down between your legs. With a swift swing, move the dumbbell out in front of you to either chin height or, if the weight is very light, over your head in a standing position. Then let the dumbbell swing down while you crouch back to the starting position. Exhale as you swing up and inhale as you swing down. Do sets of 12 to 20.

LEGS

Legs lose their shape rather quickly after the school years, despite their degree of development in strength or tone. Leg work is important because it speeds up your metabolism, burns up numerous calories in high repetitions, and helps to increase our whole body's strength. In fact, leg work alone would help to shape up your entire body and also tone you up.

In weight training, I see too many trainers concentrating on building up their upper bodies and neglecting their legs. When I asked them why they were not working their legs, they replied that they were running for their legs. Though running is great for general body tone and cardiovascular conditioning, it is not sufficient for leg buildup. Olympic sprinters have outstanding legs from sprint workouts which quickly contract the muscles and build them up. They also perform weight workouts. Long-distance runners follow incredible workouts of very long runs that break down their leg muscles and prohibit any size buildup. Their legs are very thin without much definition—generally not what you would want if you are striving for size.

The major muscles in the legs are the gluteus maximus (hips); the posterior thigh muscles, the majority of which are the hamstrings or "hams" or thigh biceps; the anterior thigh muscles, which are generally called the quadriceps, though they also include other muscles; and the calf, which includes two muscles: the gastrocnemius, the major part of the calf which is diamond-shaped, and the soleus, the lower part of the calf. The gastroc-soleus muscles extend into the heel bone through the Achilles heel and are responsible for ankle extension. These muscles also cross the back of the knee joint and assist the hams in knee movement.

Leg muscles must be maintained to support two important body parts: the knee and the ankle. The body's largest joint is the knee, where much of the body's weight is supported, especially for the athlete and his stop-go movements. Essentially a hinge that is held together by a system of ligaments and tendons, the knee is one of the weakest joints of the body because its bones are never in full contact with each other. Several ligaments support the knee; the important thigh and calf muscles cross over these ligaments. The powerful quadricep muscles and hamstring muscles cross the knee for a tripod effect around the joint.

Like the knee, the ankle joint is supported by strong ligaments on either side, bears most of the body's weight, and is vulnerable to injury. A multiplicity of ligaments allows the ankle mobility and stability: the medial (inside of the ankle) and lateral (outside) are the strongest ligament sets. Crossing the medial are muscle tendons that also exert force and offer support.

The squat is a basic but very effective exercise. In my opinion, it is the most beneficial exercise in all of weight training. Not only does it work the glutes, quads and hams, but it expands your rib cage and gets the blood flowing for whole body growth. Squatting helps your total strength and will even help you maximum lift in the bench press to go up. Additionally, the squat works the legs and back in unison, as your school sports once did. High repetition squats are good for cardiovascular conditioning and burn up lots of calories. But because squatting is the most taxing of all exercises, you will have to go more slowly than in the other exercises.

Squats are considered by some individuals to be dangerous to the back and knees. As long as you are first warmed up well and go down slowly, keeping your back straight, you won't hurt your back. Too quick a descension or bending over too much may be damaging, however. You shouldn't hurt your knees if you don't go parallel and refrain from bouncing on the way up.

Another criticism of squats is that they reportedly build up your butt too much. Though squats do work your glutes, they tighten them and shape them as they work the rest of your legs. In fact, squats will firm up a fatty hind end. Additionally, hack squats are beneficial exercises, especially for the quads, but they don't compare with the regular squat.

If you have knee problems, consult a sports physician about squatting, just as you would if you had another injured body part. Usually, after considerable therapy, you can return to at least partial, if not parallel, squats. Last summer, I suffered a torn anterior cruciate ligament playing handball, but after therapy, I returned to partial squats after six weeks and parallel squats after three months.

Leg extensions really bring those quads out. Use iron boots if you don't have a quad machine. Leg curls will bomb those hams. Your hams should be two-thirds as strong as your quads, so if you are using 100 pounds on your leg extensions, use between sixty-five to seventy pounds on your leg curls. A leg press is a good compound exercise—it works both the anterior and posterior thigh muscles. However, be careful because a leg press can put more strain on your knees than a squat, depending on how you use it. I have also been using the old-fashioned lunge recently. If you think your hams and lower glute tie-ins have been worked before, try this exercise, and I promise you that you will be sore (avoid this if you have knee problems).

The calves are the most difficult muscle group in the body to build up because of their constant use in walking, climbing stairs, and rising from a seated position. Because they are so difficult to build up, I recommend getting to those burns quickly: try ten burning reps—you only start counting when you start to burn—after either high reps or heavy reps, whichever works best for you. I prefer donkey-toe raises because the weight is so close to your calves. Also, they seem to pump the gastrocnemius the best. To hit the lower part of the calf, the soleus, I use a seated cal machine.

If you schedule three-day leg workouts, make certain that you have only one heavy day, one medium day, and one light day. Otherwise, you will be overtrained, which is just as easy as being undertrained.

Performing leg work with weights will help to prevent knee and other leg injuries in tennis, racquetball, and running. Eighty percent of the support for your knee comes from the quadriceps and hams; building these up reduces the chance of a serious knee injury. Leg strength developed through weight training can slightly improve your speed in tennis, racquetball, and running competitions as well. Leg work will also improve your swimming and your bicycling endurance.

I hope this chapter will encourage you to put your legs in shape. The reason I began this body-parts discussion with the legs is because I feel the legs are the most important, yet most commonly overlooked muscle group. Also, I believe that workouts should begin with the largest muscle groups. By initially working the largest muscle groups, you are following a logical and kinesiologically correct procedure. And because leg work is the most taxing of training exercises, I advise getting it done first or you might not have the strength at the end of your workout.

B1-2: Cybex Thigh Machine
(below)
Rob Lytle of the Denver Broncos shows us how to use this fine machine, which works your quadriceps when you extend your leg up and your hamstrings when you bring your leg down. You set the dial according to the intensity you want. This machine is usually used for rehabilitation of knee injuries.

A1-4: Nautilus Compound Leg Machine *(left)*
Seat yourself in the machine, knees bent and feet against the pads. Grasp the handles lightly. Extend the legs forward fully, keeping the back against the seat. Then, for the press, place feet against the pads and press the legs forward.

C1-2: Nautilus Leg Curl
Lie face down on the machine and place your feet under the roller pads with your knees just over the edge of the bench. Lightly grasp the handles to keep your body from moving and then curl your legs, trying to touch your heels to your buttocks. When your lower legs are perpendicular to the bench, lift your buttocks to increase your movement. Then pause at the point of full muscular contraction. Slowly lower your resistance and repeat the exercise.

E1: Hydra-Gym Running Machine *(right)*
Simulate a running motion while lying on your back, making sure you get the full range of motion bringing your legs all the way up, down, right, and left for 30 seconds each. This exercise will really burn up all parts of your thighs.

D1: Kaiser Cam Leg Curl
(above)
This machine works on
pneumatic principles. Just set the
resistance you want and fully
extend your leg all the way up
while you are lying flat on the
bench.

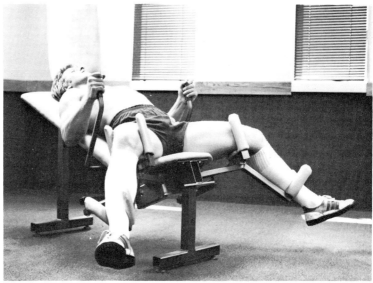

F1-2: Hydra-Gym Ad-Ab Machine *(left)*
This is great for the inner and outer parts of your thighs. In the starting position with your legs together, bring them out as fast and as hard as you can, then bring them together and repeat. Start with 2 sets of 20-seconds with a minute to rest. Then after you are broken in (after a couple of weeks), try 2 sets of 30-seconds.

G1-2: Universal Leg Press
Adjust the support chair until your legs bend as indicated. Take a deep breath and push with your legs until almost fully extended but not locked out, exhaling as you exert. Return to the starting position and repeat. If you are recuperating from knee problems, be careful — consult your physician before doing the leg press.

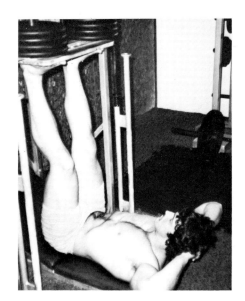

H1-2: Old-Fashioned Leg Press
Not recommended for anyone recuperating from a knee injury. Once again, fully extend the leg 12 times a set, completing 3 sets. This machine puts pressure on the knee, but it can be used in conjunction with other leg exercises.

I1: AMF Leg Press

This machine works all parts of your thigh. Start with the weight approximating your body weight; set the floor bench to your appropriate height as per the machine's instructions. Extend your legs all the way up, but don't let the weights come down all the way (just to almost touching); 12–15 reps is good to pump those thighs. Progressively add weight so that you will be aiming for twice body weight.

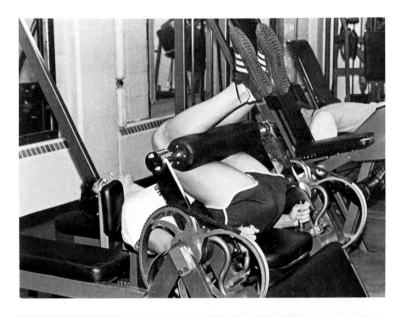

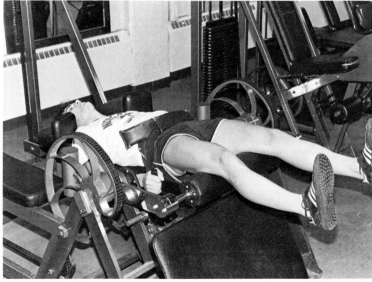

J1–2: Nautilus Hip-and-Back Machine
Lie on your back, shoulders against the pads. Strap the seat belt around your waist and grasp the handles while placing your legs over the pads so that the knees are close to the chest. Straighten your legs out while keeping the back straight.

K1-2: Squat
Place the weight behind the neck. This squat works the posterior and anterior thigh muscles, the gluteus maximus and even the rib cage. Lower yourself slowly to avoid back injury, and don't bounce off the knee. Be careful if you have knee problems; consult your physician first. You may have to do partial squats instead of complete ones (where the thighs are parallel to the ground) if you have knee problems.

L1-2: Kaiser Cam Squat Machine
Set the dial to the intensity you desire. Squat to *at least* three-quarters of the way down and explode up for 12-15 reps.

M1-2: Front Squat *(right)*
Front squats will help you strengthen your quadriceps. Start by resting the weight on your shoulders in an upright position, arms crossed to hold the barbell. Lower yourself until your thighs are parallel to the floor. Remember to keep your back straight and your head up while you lower yourself. Don't bounce into the lower position. The success of this exercise relies on lowering yourself slowly.

N1-2: Hack Squat

Grip the bar behind your back
in a downward position and
then raise up to a three-quarters
position. Then move down until
your thighs are parallel to the
ground. Make sure you come up
only three-quarters of the way.
This exercise pumps the
quadriceps (anterior thigh
muscles) as well as some
posterior thigh muscles
effectively. Some bodybuilders
prefer this exercise to the regular
squat because it does not work
your glutes.

O1-2: Bar Lunge

Stand straight up with the bar resting on your back. Extend one leg forward and bend down until the opposite leg is almost touching the ground. Then stand up straight and lunge forward with the other leg. This exercise effectively pumps your thighs, especially the glute-ham tie-in.

P1-3: Side Jump
Rest the bar on your back and, while raising your legs one at a time, jump sideways over a bench. Then reverse the jump. You should do this in sets of 20. Make sure you start with a light weight and low bench. This exercise will work your abductors, adductors, and help your lateral speed.

Q1-2: Step-Up
This is as easy as walking up and down the stairs. With weight in position as pictured, just step up and down on a step.

 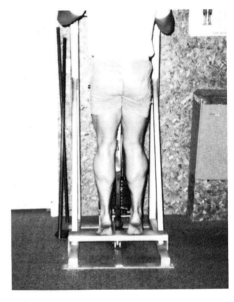

R1: Donkey Toe Raise

Donkey toe raises are more difficult than toe raises because of the weight's closer proximity to the calves. Have a partner sit on your back as you brace yourself over a table. Thrust upward onto your toes a minimum of 20 repetitions a set. You should feel that good "burning sensation" in the calves at least 10 times to utilize this exercise effectively.

S1: Toe Raise

The calves are the target of this exercise performed using this toe-raise machine. The development of the calves can increase a player's speed and quickness, and toe raises work on the calves with quick result. Try for a full extension as you thrust upward onto your toes. Do this exercise in sets of 20.

T1: Nautilus Toe Raise

Strap yourself around the waist and adjust the resistance. Grasp the handle as indicated while raising and lowering yourself slowly.

U1-2: Seated Calf-Toe Raise
(below)

Wedge your knees under the padded bar and move your heels up and down as far as possible. This exercise works your soleus, or the lower part of your calves. make sure you do at least 10 burning reps.

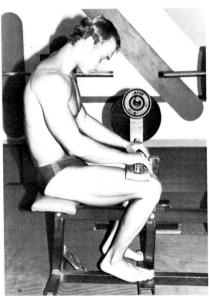

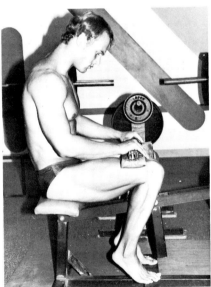

BACK

Many back problems can be prevented and solved by including back work in your routine. I see many men in their twenties who already suffer from lower back problems. Also, have you ever noticed a weight lifter who has a great chest with seemingly sloped shoulders? Probably too little back work in relation to his overdeveloped chest has actually pushed his shoulders and traps to make him appear slope-shouldered (some pull-downs are not sufficient; he needs rowing and possibly pull-tos).

The strongest and largest back muscles are the latissmus dorsi or "lats." These powerful muscles need to be worked at every angle. Wide-grip pulley pull-downs or side-grip chin-ups work the width of the lats. To build the lower lats, try narrow-grip chin-ups or pulley pull-downs with a narrow grip. Work the middle area of the back with bent-over parallel barbell rows or dumbbell rows. T-bar rows are a favorite of mine and are great for building thickness on the outside part of the lats. An added advantage to doing dumbbell rows and seated pulley rows is that they also build the posterior head of the deltoids, which is usually neglected.

As I mentioned above, the lower back causes many problems — probably because it is usually the most neglected area of the body. It needs to be strong to prevent injuries from heavy lifting. Too many bodybuilders have suffered needless lower-back injuries by training with heavy weights overhead without first having built up their lower back muscles, the spinal erectors. If the bodybuilder has a healthy back, I prefer starting him out on hyperextensions, first on a flat bench, then later off a Roman chair or bench. I also like doing good-morning exercises for the spinal erectors. After six weeks to three months of these basics, I recommend dead lifts. These work the legs and the back in conjunction, and are a great power exercise. Dead lifts coordinate the entire set of back muscles in one lift as well as improving the grip, forearms, and traps. I have included stiff-legged dead lifts in the back chapter for simplicity, but they really bomb the hamstrings (Robby Robinson claims they are the key to his great hams). I do not usually recommend cleans for the bodybuilder, because they require so much skill and can result in injury if not performed correctly. However, cleans are an incredible exercise for strengthening the whole back, and in sports they extend explosive power. I recommend that if you do them, have an expert supervise you, and start very light to prevent injury.

Lastly, back work will improve your time and endurance in swimming, in addition to helping your tennis and racquetball swing—enabling you to hit the ball harder, and giving you a more effective serve and return. Most importantly, back work will allow you to feel and look better.

A1: Shrug
Grasp the dumbbells with your palms facing inward. Let your shoulders fall down, and then raise the shoulders without moving your arms.

B1: Upright row
Grasp the barbell with a narrow
grip and raise the bar to a
position even with your
shoulders. Hold the bar in this
position for a second or two
while keeping your elbows
pointed outwards. Repeat this
exercise 12 times in 3 different
sets.

C1-2: Nautilus Shrug
Adjust the machine so that when
you bend your elbows at right
angles while sitting on the seat,
you can place your forearms in
the padded blocks as shown.
Keeping your arms stiff, pull up
by the shoulders.

D1-3: Nautilus Compound Back Machine

Adjust the seat so that your shoulder joints are in line with the axis of the cams and fasten the seat belt. For the *pullover,* press the foot pedal until the elbow pads are about chin level. Place your elbows on the pads, your hands open and resting on the curved portion of the bar. Remove your foot and slowly rotate your elbows as far back as possible, then down until the bar touches your stomach. Pause. For the *pulldown,* lean forward and grasp the overhead bar with a parallel grip. Keeping your elbows back, pull the bar down. Pause.

E1–2: Pulldown
Set the weight, sit down, and pull the bar, holding it with a wide grip, down to your neck. Do 12 reps.

F1: Bent-over Parallel Row
Hold the bar with a wide grip while you bend over, parallel to the ground. Pull the bar upward until it strikes you in the chest, and then lower the bar slowly. This will develop the latissimus dorsi.

G1: One-Arm Dumbbell Row
Keep both legs stiff and one arm
placed on a bench or chair.
Extend the dumbbell fully
downwards and then lift it back
up till it hits your chest.
Remember to keep the legs stiff
and avoid cheating by bending
your knees. This exercise should
be repeated 12 times in sets of 3.

H1-2: T-Bar Row

Upward T-bar rows give the lats
more power. Hold your hands
on the bar and let the bar drop
as you keep your back and
knees slightly bent. In a
linebacker position, pull the bar
up to your chest — being mindful
of the full range of
motion — letting the bar all the
way down slowly and then
pulling it to your chest. The
form and the motion are more
important than the amount of
weight. Be careful not to use too
heavy a weight at first. Also,
avoid using your back — just the
pulling motion.

I1-2: Cable Row

Stand in a stooped position with a cable in each hand. At a few paces away from the plates, extend your arms fully and pull them to your chest. Return to the starting position. You may also do this seated. As with the cable bar rows, this will work your lats and the posterior head of your deltoids.

J1: Behind-the-Neck Chin-Up
This type of chin-up will develop your lats, deltoids, and general back area. Use a wide grip and raise yourself until the back of your head touches the bar.

K1-2: Barbell Clean
With your legs spread to shoulder width, grasp the bar so that your palms face the floor. Your thighs should be almost parallel to the floor as you explode into the next position illustrated. With your elbows pointing straight in front of you, spring off the floor onto the balls of your feet as you lift the bar to your shoulders.

L1–4: Dumbbell Clean and Press

This is the most complete and important upper-body exercise possible with weights – an almost complete body exercise. Start by crouching in an almost seated position. Begin to clean the dumbbells by raising them over your shoulders. As soon as the dumbbells reach the top of your ankles, try to spring onto the balls of your feet to complete the motion. Next, press the dumbbells either simultaneously or by alternating arms.

M1: Back Hyperextension *(above)*

This exercise will require a partner. Keep your hands behind your head as your partner holds your calves down. Surge backwards, arching your back to hyperextend yourself. This will strengthen the lower back and should be done in 3 sets of 20 to 25 repetitions.

N1-2: Good-Morning Exercise
Start with an empty bar when
you begin and then gradually
build up the amount of weight
you use. Place the bar behind
your back from a standing
position and then bend over
until your back is parallel to the
floor. Be sure that you are using
a light amount of weight to
avoid back strain. Build your
routine up to 2 to 3 sets of 10 to
15 repetitions.

O1: Dead Lift

After you have performed the good-morning exercise for a few weeks, move on to the dead lift. Address the bar with a grip slightly wider than your leg spread. Hold the bar with one palm facing frontwards and the other backwards. Bend over and lift the bar to your waist, while keeping your arms straight. As you get the bar to this position, thrust your shoulders back and your chest out. This should be performed with a light weight for the first few weeks, until the spinal erectors are strengthened.

First try 15 reps. Then as your development progresses, you can decrease the reps and increase the amount of weight.

P1-2: Stiff-legged Deadlift

Stand on an elevated platform holding the bar and with your legs almost completely stiff. Bend down till the barbells go below the platform. Your back should be at least parallel, if not lower; then stand straight up. Make sure you have really warmed up your back and legs first. Avoid this exercise if you have a back problem.

Q1: Straddle
Straddle the bar as you squat
down to grip the bar with one
palm up and one down. Then
just stand up, being careful to
keep your back straight as you
bring the bar to your crotch.
Then return to the starting
position and repeat.

DELTOIDS

The shoulders play an essential role because they coordinate movement between the torso and arms and, consequently, between whole body movements. Shoulder muscles transfer body power into the arms. Aside from their obvious importance in athletics, broad shoulders are considered by many to be an essence of manhood as exemplified by the oft-heard statement: "Shoulders make the man." Most individuals are not born with great shoulders, they must work at it. The bodybuilder's deltoids evolve to an incredible size after hours of training. Once the shoulders have been developed, whether now or back in high school, the young man needs to work regularly on his shape and tone.

The most important of the eleven muscles that produce shoulder joint movement is the aforementioned deltoid. A triangular muscle, the deltoid is on the shoulder—one angle points down the arm, the two others bend around the front and rear of the shoulder. The deltoid muscle's three heads have three different functions: the anterior (front head) lifts the arm forward; the lateral (side head) lifts them sideways; and the posterior (rear head) lifts them backwards.

The anterior head is most easily built up, because it is worked in any pressing movement. The lateral head is more difficult to work, but responds well to lateral raises as well as to a few other exercises; the lateral heads make your shoulders look broader. The posterior heads are the most difficult to build up and are usually the most neglected. You can build them up by performing behind-the-neck presses, bent-over lateral raises, reverse incline flies, and behind-the-neck chin-ups. Those of you in competition form will be able to see the definition between the different deltoid heads.

Most trap exercises, especially upright rows, work the deltoids in addition to the back (see the back chapter). Also, any kind of press—bench press, incline press or decline press—works the deltoids.

For athletes, I usually stress the power movements like presses for deltoid development. Though all presses are compound exercises, they work many muscle groups. For those of you who are more advanced lifters and are interested in working toward a super physique rather than just shaping up, I recommend supersetting all of the front, lateral, and bent-over dumbbell raises together to guarantee a blowup of all of your delts. Also, I occasionally have my advance trainees superset upright rows with the dumbbell raises or presses with the dumbbell raises. When you do the dumbbell raises followed by an immediate superset with the military press, you are employing again the pre-exhaust training technique.

In sports, built-up shoulders will put power in your racquetball and tennis swing, and help you swim faster and longer. Track men have been using weights for years to improve their running. Notice the way your arms move when you run properly and how tired your shoulders become—proof enough that increased deltoid strength will help your running both in speed and in endurance.

A1: Front Deltoid Raise
These raises are designed to develop the anterior deltoids. Start in a standing position and grip the dumbbells, using a palms-up technique. Raise the dumbbells until they are even with the shoulders and then continue to raise them directly overhead. Be careful not to bend your elbows while performing this exercise so as not to take away from the usefulness of the movement.

B1: Bent-over Lateral Raise
The posterior deltoids are the
object of this exercise. Bend over
until your back is parallel to the
floor. Use a palms-down grip to
lift the dumbbells till they are
even with your shoulders.
Conclude the movement by
slowly lowering the dumbbells
back to their starting position.

C1-2: Standing Lateral Raise
Stand up with your arms
extended downward and with
your palms facing each other.
Raise the dumbbells to your side
and above your shoulders. This
exercise does a good job of
pumping the lateral, or side,
head of your deltoids.

D1: Overhand Chin-Up

This chin-up develops all three
heads of the deltoids. Grip the
bar with an overhand grip,
standing sidways beneath the
bar. Pull yourself up until your
chin touches the bar and then
repeat the chin-up — this time
bringing your head up on the
opposite side of the bar.

E1-2: Seated, Behind-the-Neck Military Press

The deltoids and triceps are the target of the sitting military press. From the seated position, rest the barbell on the back of your shoulders. Press the barbell upwards, remembering to exhale as you begin your press.

F1-2: Standing Military Press
(below)

This variation is similar to the seated press but can be done from a position on the front or back of the shoulders. From a clean position, press the bar straight up from the shoulders.

G1–2: Standing Dumbbell Press
From a clean position, press the dumbbells either one at a time or together straight up from the shoulders.

H1–4: Nautilus Double Shoulder Machine *(right)*
Adjust the seat so that your shoulder joints are in line with the axis of the cams. Fasten the seat belt. For the *lateral movement*, pull the handles back till your knuckles touch the pads. Lead with your elbows and raise both your arms till they are parallel with the floor. Pause. Slowly lower your resistance and repeat. For the *press*, grasp the handles above your shoulders and press overhead. Do not arch your back.

I1: Jerk
While in the clean position (balancing the barbell on a vertical line with your shoulders, as shown), thrust the barbell upwards from the shoulder position, scissoring your legs. Then hold the barbell up while bringing the legs together. This is a great shoulder, leg, back, trap, and forearm exercise. It is also an Olympic lift. But be careful; go light. Not all gyms will allow you to do this exercise because it is dangerous.

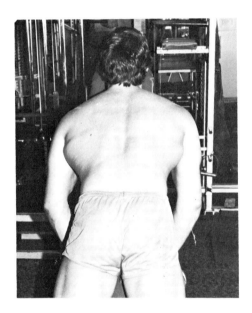

J1-2: Reverse Incline Fly
Lie on an incline bench face down, holding the dumbbells with your palms facing each other. Extend your arms up and out at shoulder length. This is an advanced exercise for your lateral and posterior deltoids.

CHEST

As men steer away from their youth, their chests tend to lose firmness and their pectoral muscles soften. These developments can be rectified by a good program of proper diet and appropriate training exercises with such equipment as dumbbells or cable flies.

The chest is probably a close second to the arms in popularity for training. Manliness and big chests have long been equated. The largest part of the chest and the most important of the numerous muscles that surround the chest area are the pectorals, major and minor. The pectoralis major lies across the front of the chest and is large and fan-shaped. One end of this muscle is attached to the front of the upper arm, the other is attached to the sternum. The upper arms are moved across the body when the pectoral muscles contract.

The rib cage and the serratus magnus, a three-fingered muscle attached thereto, are also considered part of the chest. Many trainers believe that a rib cage (actually, the cartilage) can't be expanded past the age of twenty-one so they don't stress rib-cage-expansion exercises like the pull-over for adult men. I believe that the rib cage can be expanded well past twenty-one, but I doubt whether you will be able to expand it after thirty-five.

Bench presses are included in this section for the sake of simplicity. The bench press is an upper-body compound exercise that develops most of your upper body, primarily the deltoid, triceps, and the major part of your pectorals. In my opinion, however, it is not the greatest exercise specifically for the chest. Only 30–38% of the bench press works the pecs. The variation is in the hand placement—the wider out, the more you work your pecs, the closer in, the more you work your triceps. The bench press generally works the deltoids and triceps. A side benefit of the close-grip bench press, which I have included under arms, is its work on the interior part of the pecs.

A massive chest could be developed with two exercises alone: the incline press, preferably with dumbbells, and the forward dip. The incline press works the upper pec, besides deltoids and triceps, and the forward dip works the lower pec as well as the outside of the pecs. The decline press is a supplementary exercise to develop the lower pecs. I recommend an angle of about 38% in the incline. An angle of 45% or more gives you too much deltoid development and too little upper pec.

Flies square off your chest and will really improve a chest that is beginning to lose its shape. Mix up all variety of flies, incline, flat, decline, cables, crossovers, etc. Of course, you wouldn't do all types of flies at once, but through the routines you can mix them up so as to work all parts of your chest. For very advanced trainees, I like to superset flies with inclines or declines. By exhausting the pecs initially with the flies, then following immediately with the compound exercise (no more than four seconds before each movement) like the inclines or declines, you get a real pump. The congestion from using this pre-exhaust principle is amazing. Advanced trainees can use this principle with almost any muscle groups by first doing the isolation exercise, then immediately following with the compound exercise.

You should be careful not to overtrain in your chest work. Its popularity makes this very tempting. You don't want to do twenty sets three times a week for the chest unless you want little improvement and possibly retrogression. Don't forget: you want your body to look symmetrical—your chest should fit well with the rest of your body. A huge, defined chest on an otherwise undeveloped body would be an absurdity.

Those of you that swim will find that not only your breast stroke improves when you develop your chest, but so does your freestyle swimming. The pectorals are used in all swimming motions. In racquetball and tennis, backhand shots will be improved by pec development.

A1: Bench Press

Grasp the bar at shoulder width
and bring the bar down to the
top of your pectorals with an
inhaling breath; then press the
bar upwards as you exhale until
you can fully extend and lock
your arms. Do not arch your
back or buttocks but remain in
contact with the bench at all
times. Your feet should be flat
on the floor. Rob Lytle is shown
benching 365 lbs. as Coach Dave
Preston looks on.

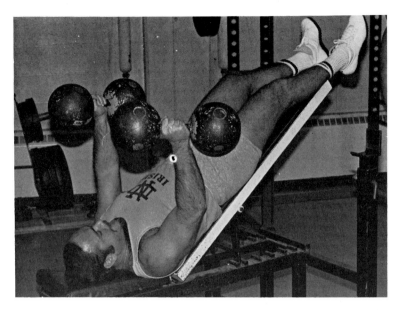

B1: Barbell Incline press *(left)*
While at a 45° angle, press the bar upward with an exhaling breath, pausing to lock your arms in an extended position, and then lower the bar back down to the top of your pectorals. The incline press is also beneficial for building the pectoral-deltoid tie-in — an area of the upper chest that the bench press does not develop.

C1: Dumbbell Incline Press *(left)*
This exercise strengthens the upper pectorals and triceps. It is especially effective for the pectoral-deltoid tie-in. Starting with the dumbbells wide apart yet touching your shoulders, press the dumbbells upwards until they are straight up and closer together than at the start.

D1: Dumbbell Decline Press
(above)
This exercise works the lower pectorals as well as the anterior head of the deltoids and triceps. You reverse your position from the incline, thereby having your head at the bottom and feet in the air. Hold the dumbbells wide at the base, touching your shoulders, and press them up, narrow at the top. Pete Broccoletti is seen here using 100-pound dumbbells. You should start with less weight.

E1-4 Easy-Curl Pullover and Dumbbell Pullover
Lying either straight or across a bench with your head over the edge, pull the bar off the ground over your head to a position over the top of your pectorals, keeping the hip in contact with the bench and the bar or dumbbell from touching your pecs. Avoid using heavy weights for the pullover, for this will cause you to cheat by bending the elbows. Keep the rib cage relaxed, so you can stretch the entire rib structure.

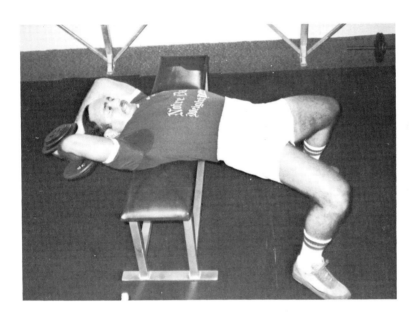

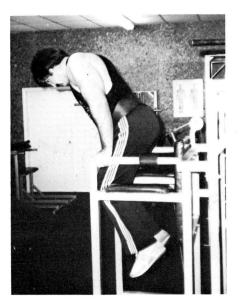

F1-4: Nautilus Compound Chest Machine *(left)*
Sit firmly in the chair and place your feet on the front pads. Put your forearms behind the pec-deck pads, grasping the handles. Smoothly bring the arms together, then apart. Now for the press portion of the exercise, rest your legs on the flat pads, grasping the press handles. Then press forward.

G1-2: Forward Dip *(above)*
Lean forward and proceed to press yourself upwards while maintaining the forward lean. This will add bulk to the upper body and chest. You may use a dumbbell to weight yourself down.

H1-2: Flat Fly *(left)*
While lying flat on the bench with a dumbbell in each hand, extend your arms below the bench with your elbows slightly bent. Bring the two dumbbells up toward your chest (two-thirds of the way). You do not want to bring the dumbbells together because this would take the tension off. This exercise works to square off your middle pectorals (the major part of your chest) and the front and side heads of your deltoids.

I1-2: Lying Crossover Fly
While lying on a flat bench, extend your arms below the bench with your elbows slightly bent. Bring the dumbbells accross your chest so that they cross each other. This is a more advanced exercise than the regular flat fly.

J1-2: Incline Fly

This exercise works the outer pectoral muscles. Keep your elbows bent slightly, and bring the dumbbells two-thirds to three-quarters of the way up across the chest. Don't lift the dumbbells all the way up until they touch, for that would release the tension on the outer pecs and minimize the efficiency of the exercise.

K1-2: Decline Fly (right)

At an angle of about 40°, extend your arms out as far as they can go, then bring them toward your chest middle until they are about three-quarters of the way together. make sure you are secure in the decline bench. This really squares your lower and outer chest.

L1-3: Crossover Cable

In this exercise, you should be seated with your hands holding a cable. Extend your arms out fully to the side and bring the cables across your chest so that they cross each other. This is another advanced exercise that will square off your chest and pump your deltoids.

NECK

The definition of a healthy appearance includes a full neck, unlike the haggard, weak-looking neck characteristic of illness. Though not numerous, the neck's muscles are very significant, especially as a type of shock absorber for the athlete's shoulders and head. A strong neck prevents minor injuries such as whiplash, pulled neck muscles, and a stiff neck, too.

The neck is a musculature that protects the seven small cervical vertebrae upon which man's head is balanced. Along with spinal ligaments, the neck muscles play a key restraining role in opposing sudden neck movement. The majority of the neck's mass is comprised of about fifteen small- and medium-sized muscles that can produce movement in seven different directions:

1. Elevating the shoulders
2. Bending the head toward the chest
3. Drawing the head backward
4. Bending the head down toward the right shoulder
5. Bending the head down toward the left shoulder
6. Twisting the head to look over the right shoulder
7. Twisting the head to look over the left shoulder

The neck is probably the easiest part of the body to build up because its muscles are seldom worked out. In fact, neck muscles respond immediately when a full-range exercise program is provided for the above seven functions. Whenever you strain, such as in presses, with forced reps, you are indirectly building the neck up. Unless you are still playing football, hockey or wrestling, and you need a powerful, well-developed neck for protection, a too large neck is not preferable because of its unaesthetic appearance. Most bodybuilders do not specifically exercise their necks so as not to upset their symmetrical look.

For those who no longer play sports that require a large neck, the indirect stimulus that your neck acquires from shrugs, upright rows, and the forced reps in the presses are more than sufficient to build your neck up adequately. However, for those of you who feel you have small necks and want quick neck development, I recommend either the Nautilus 4-way neck machine or the Hydra Gym neck machine. At Notre Dame and with the Denver Broncos, I saw some men add an inch or more in three weeks with these machines.

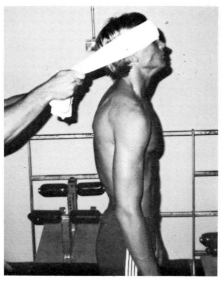

A1-2: Towel Neck Exercise

First start by having your partner place the towel behind the back of your neck and apply pressure toward the front. Try to touch the back of your head to your back while the tension is being applied. Now try the same exercise with the towel on the back of the head and at each side. Attempt to move your head in the opposite direction of the tension, bringing your head forward to your chest or your ear to your shoulder.

B1-4: Isometric Neck Exercise

This exercise will put constant pressure on the neck muscles while the exerciser is leaning into the arms of his partner or being lifted by his partner's hands. The neck muscles are doing the work supporting the person's weight into top sequence. Just stand stiff and lean into your partner, allowing all your weight to be supported by the neck muscles. Do in all four directions. In the bottom sequence, simply resist the upward or downward pressure of your partner.

C1: Isometric Neck Exercise (with partner's legs) *(above)*
Here the partner remains stationary while you put pressure against his legs. Remember to do both sides.

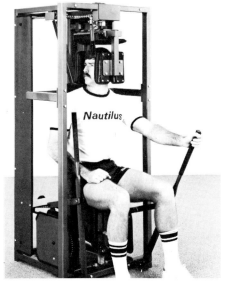

D1: Nautilus Neck Rotator Machine *(right)*
Grasp the handles as indicated after putting the neck in place and setting the tension to the desired resistance. Turn the head the full range of motion from left to right and back.

E1: Wrestler's Bridge

Place your feet flat and firm as you bridge yourself up so that your feet and head are the only parts of your body in contact with the floor. When you reach this position, roll back, forth, and sideways to get the most out of the exercise.

F1: Neck harness *(right)*

Bend your back as you stand in a crouched position. Lower your head and then raise it, utilizing your neck muscles only. Be careful not to use too much weight in this exercise — usually 20 pounds is plenty.

G1-4: Nautilus 4-Way Neck Machine
(posterior extension)
Adjust the seat so your Adam's apple is in line with the axis of the cam. The back of your head should contact the middle of the pads. Stabilize your torso by lightly grasping the handles. Extend your head as far back as possible and pause. Slowly return to the stretched position and repeat.

(anterior flexion)
Face the machine and adjust the seat so your nose is in the center of the pads. Stabilize your torso by lightly gripping the handles. Smoothly move your head toward your chest. pause. Then slowly return to the stretched position and repeat.

(lateral contraction)
Your left ear should be in the
center of the pads. Stabilize
your torso by lightly grasping
the handles. Smoothly move
your head towad your left
shoulder. Pause. Keep your
shoulders square and then
slowly return to the stretched
position and repeat. Reverse the
procedure for the right side.

H1–4: Hydra-Gym Neck Machine

For the front-to-back exercise (H1-2), place your face about midway of the two front pads and adjust the machine to fit snugly. The chest should be tight against the bottom pad. Push back with the back of the head till you reach the maximum backward flexion. Then push directly forward into the pads until you reach the maximum forward flexion. For the side-to-side exerciser (H3-4), place the head about midway between the two sets of pads (you should be able to see just over the bar that holds the cylinders) and adjust the head

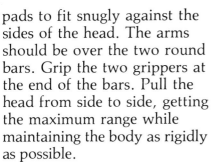

pads to fit snugly against the sides of the head. The arms should be over the two round bars. Grip the two grippers at the end of the bars. Pull the head from side to side, getting the maximum range while maintaining the body as rigidly as possible.

ARMS & WRISTS

Men, no matter what age, seem to want big arms. Young men especially correlate big arms with strength—which is not necessarily true. Your bone structure determines the maximum size to which you can develop your arms "naturally." If you have a 6½-inch wrist, you have a small bone structure; if you have a 7–7½-inch wrist, you have a medium-size bone structure; and an 8-inch or bigger size wrist indicates you have a large bone structure. Body classifications are ectomorph or thin-type, endomorph or heavy set, and mesomorph or naturally athletic. If you have a small bone structure, you can make bodybuilding gains with an extra effort. A nicely sized arm is one which is developed to nine inches more than the wrist size. I believe that the maximum you can naturally develop your upper arms is eleven inches larger than your wrist.

Two large muscles and thirteen smaller ones control the flexing and extending of the elbow joint. The most important muscle of the eight flexion muscles is the biceps; the most important muscle of the seven extension muscles is the triceps.

The bicep is a prominent, two-headed muscle, and when developed to the maximum, each head can be clearly and separately defined. Down the center of the biceps runs a thick vein (cephalic). The shoulder and the elbow are crossed by the biceps. The three functions of the biceps are: elbow flexing, lifting the upper arm forward, and hand supinating or outward rotation.

When you train your biceps, you should not only be concerned with size, but peak and thickness through the width of the muscle. Between the biceps and the triceps is the brachialis, which can add size to your arms.

In comparison to the biceps, however, the triceps comprise a larger part of the arm—60%. The tricep tendons also cross both the elbow joint and the shoulder. The two-fold function of the triceps is to straighten the elbow and to assist in bring down the upper arm from an overhead position. The triceps have three heads: (1) inner (medial) head, (2) outer head, and (3) long head. All of these heads should be worked to attain that horseshoe look on your triceps and to develop your arm to its potential. The small muscle between the bicep origin and the tricep origin at the deltoid is the coracobrachialis, which is worked indirectly by presses.

The forearm is a complex structure composed of nineteen separate muscles that involve the fingers and the wrist. Aside from the flexion of the forearm against the upper arm—a bicep function, the forearm's functions are: gripping, finger extension, hand supination (outward rotation), hand pronation (inwards rotation), and bending the hand in four separate directions.

I place bicep exercises along with lats in my bodybuilding programs for intermediate and advanced trainees.

My bodybuilding programs for intermediate and advanced trainees place bicep exercises along with lats. I, like many others, used to train the biceps and triceps together, but when doing it on a six-day routine, I found I was not getting enough recuperation time. Whenever you work your lats, you also get some bicep work, so I was really overtraining my biceps and triceps. I was also having elbow problems. Combining my biceps with my lats has not only had great results, but since trying this, I have had no elbow problems. These elbow problems were because of all the tricep work. In all presses you get tricep work, so in reality, I was getting some tricep and bicep work six days a week! No wonder the tendons in my elbows were sore. You will also note from my workouts that I prefer dumbbells in my training. Using dumbbells in your curls will give you equal development in the arms, whereas with a bar, one arm will compensate for the other. Doing dumbbell incline curls will give you the stretch that is a key to bicep form and fullness. When you use a barbell, there is a tendency to not only cheat but to get too much deltoid. Preacher curls, which were popularized by the great Larry Scott and often called Scott curls, are great for working the lower biceps. If you have a great peak but no lower bicep developed, you are deficient—get on those preacher curls. However, if you have a problem with sore elbows (tendonitis), avoid that exercise like the plague. If you use 100 pounds on a preacher curl, you have 20,000 pounds of pressure per square inch on your elbows; no wonder it may cause elbow problems. I particularly like concentration curls for peaking my biceps. With many of my other curls, I like doing partial reps through the middle range of motion for peaking.

Before you work your triceps, make sure you warm them up very well. Elbow problems sometimes arise from tricep extensions when you are not properly warmed up. I like dumbbell tricep extensions because they hit all three heads of the tricep. Most of all I like the tricep bench press. I personally prefer pressing movements to leverage movements anyway. The side advantage of tricep (or close grip) benches is that they will shoot up your regular bench, and the pump is tremendous. There are hundreds of tricep exercises, but because of the space limitations I have included only some of my favorites. Remember you get some tricep work in all your presses, so do not overtrain but do hit all heads.

The forearms are worked by doing reverse curls and wrist curls. One of the advantages to doing dumbbell curls is that a secondary muscle group usually being worked is the forearm. Some people do little or nothing for their forearms, feeling that they get enough indirect work from curls, etc. Grip the dumbbells harder, and you get more forearm work.

Runners should be concerned with building up their arms for endurance and speed. Track teams often have their runners do sideways curls with dumbbells, simulating the running motion for arm strength. Swimmers constantly use their arms in their strokes; thus, improved arm strength will not only help endurance but also speed.

Wrist curls and reverse curls will help your serves and returns in tennis and racquetball. However, it is important to develop your wrists, forearms, and arms to prevent elbow problems, such as tendonitis ("tennis elbow") and elbow hyperextension. Aside from warming up, building up supporting muscle groups for the elbow is the most effective way to thwart elbow problems.

A1-4; Standing or Seated Tricep Extension *(left)*

Choose whichever position is more comfortable for you. Start by gripping the dumbbell with both hands. Lower it behind your head as low as it will go. Slowly press the dumbbell over your head, making sure that your elbows are pointed inwards as you press upwards.

B1-2: One-Arm French Curl *(above)*

Again you can choose a standing or sitting position. Grasp the dumbbell in a palms-up grip with the dumbbell horizontal to the floor. Lift it over your shoulder, twisting it so that it is now in a vertical position. Drop the dumbbell behind the shoulder, remembering to keep your arm and elbow pointed straight ahead. Complete the exercise by pressing the dumbbell straight over your shoulders.

C1: Straight Dip *(above)*
Remain straight on the parallel bars and lower yourself till your shoulders and the bars are almost even. Then press straight up till you reach your starting position again.

D1-2: Lying Tricep Extension *(right)*
In a prone position, grip the easy-curl bar with your hands close together. Hold the bar over your forehead and press it upwards to a position directly over your chest. Make sure you extend your arms completely.

F1: Cable Tricep Pull *(below)*
Although the model is shown using a towel here, you can use a small bent bar if you choose. Take a few steps forward from the cable and extend your arms all the way back. Bring the towel at least two-thirds of the way forward, well past your head. This exercise effectively bombs your triceps.

E1-2: Close-Grip Bench Press *(left)*
Use a narrow grip, and lower the bar to your lower pectoral area. Keep your back in contact with the bench as you explode and press the bar into the air.

G1-2: Tricep Kick
Bend over at your waist till your back is almost parallel to the ground. While holding a dumbbell in your hands and keeping your upper arms parallel to the ground, slowly straighten your arms back. Then bring the dumbbell to the starting position and repeat.

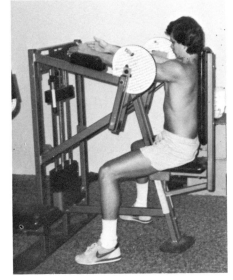

H1-2: Nautilus Tricep
Place the forearms behind the
pads in a curled position as
indicated. Keeping the top of the
arm still, rotate the forearms
down until fully extended.
Slowly return.

I1-2: Tricep Pushdown
Stand erect, narrow grip on bar, palms down or up, and elbows fixed at your sides. Take a deep breath and force the bar down till the arm is fully extended. Exhale. Return.

J1: One-Arm Concentrated Curl
(right)
Start with a palms-up grip; touch your upper arm to the same-side leg. Proceed to curl the dumbbell until you touch your shoulder.

K1-2: Dumbbell Incline Curl
Lie on an incline bench, grasping the dumbbells with a palms-forward position, dumbbells hanging by your side. While keeping the elbow as still as possible, curl the dumbbell to your shoulder.

L1: Standing Bar Curl
Grip the straight bar in a wide
or narrow grip while standing
straight. Curl the bar to your
shoulders. If you are using a
heavy weight, you can cheat by
bending your back slightly. But
be careful. This exercise puts
strain on the lower back.

M1-2: Standing Easy Curl
With back straight, stand stiffly
and with arms held close in,
simply curl straight up to your
shoulders from the down
position. You may cheat a little
on the last repetition, but be
careful, for you could hurt your
back by doing so.

N1-2: Preacher Curl

Rest your elbows on the preacher bench with the arms fully extended. Curl up toward your shoulder. This will fill in the lower part of your bicep. It is also called the Scott curl after Larry Scott, who popularized it. Avoid if you have tendonitis.

O1-2: Supinating Curl

In this exercise, you should be lying on an incline bench with your arms extended down, glued to your sides. Curl the dumbbells almost to your shoulders. make sure the bench is at a 45° angle with your feet elevated. Notice how the model is supinating, or turning, the dumbbells as he brings them up toward his shoulder. This turning up of the dumbbells gives an extra peak to your biceps. The stretch you get from the incline dumbbells greatly builds up your biceps.

P1-2: Pronating Curl
Preferably from an incline bench, hold the dumbbells while at the fully stretched-down position with your palms facing up. As you curl the dumbbells up, turn them at your hip so that when you reach the top of the movement, your palms will be facing down and slightly out. This is both a peaking movement as well as being great for the forearms.

Q1-4: Wrist Curl *(right)*
These curls will strengthen the wrists and forearms. You should do these exercises with both a palms-down position and a palms-up position. For the down position, relax the wrists so that they drop as far as they will go, then flex and raise your wrists as high as you can. For the up position, rest your forearms on your thighs and allow the bar to drop to the end of your fingers and then roll your fingers up, grabbing the bar in your palms again. Conclude by flexing your wrists as high as you can.

R1-2: Wrist Curl, Flip Flop
(above)
Hold a dumbbell with the palms up and the forearm resting on your leg. Flip the wrist so that the dumbbell and your palm are facing down. Repeat to the starting position and do sets of 15 reps.

S1-2: Sideways Curl
With your arm resting on your
knee or a bench, holding the
dumbbell sideways, extend the
dumbbell fully up and down.

T 1-3: Reverse Curl *(right)*
Take your choice of using either an easy-curl bar or a dumbbell. Holding either with a narrow or wide palms-down grip, curl it to your shoulders. These curls are aimed at developing the forearms.

U1-2: Nautilus Compound Arm Machine
To use the machine for a curl, place the elbows on the pads as indicated, grasping the bar. Curl up.

V1: Nautilus One-Arm Curl
(right)
Adjust and sit in the chair as indicated, placing the elbow against the pad and grasping the handle. Curl toward your head.

ABDOMINALS

Like many young men your age, you are probably noticing recent developments in your abdominal area—softening developments, not tightening developments. Yes, that middle-aged spread comes earlier than middle age. You no longer have a flat stomach to take for granted. Our primary concern is to firm up the abdominals and keep them in shape despite the body's tendency to naturally expand at the midsection.

Abdominal muscles make the difference in looking fit. A well-developed chest and powerful arm muscles can't mask a pot belly. Though the majority of us can't have award-winning abdominal cuts (definition), we can tighten up to an extent.

In addition to a healthy diet, plenty of work is required to get those abdominal cuts. Some bodybuilders have had great success with lower reps (25) and high-intensity exercises, such as sit-ups on a very steep incline or crunches. On the other hand, many bodybuilders have met success with very high repetitions of basic knee-bent sit-ups, elevated leg raises and Roman chair sit-ups. Use the exercise that works best for you; only you can instinctively know.

Good abdominal exercises that I prefer are: angle sit-ups on a Roman chair (for the obliques as well as the rectus abdominus), hanging frogs (for the lower abdominals), and the jack knife. Try different exercises for the lower and upper abdominals as well as for the obliques. Experiment and find which works best.

Doing abdominal work is a good warm-up before a workout and a good way to cool down along with stretching. One stretching exercise, the bar twists, also works your abs.

As you do your sit-ups, it may be encouraging to know that abdominal work will help your general conditioning, circul-respiratory condition, alleviate constipation, and prevent hernias. If you haven't done ab work recently, go slowly. The soreness after a first bout with sit-ups is quite unlike any other soreness. And if you are just starting up, try only ten to fifteen reps during the first few workout; then build up gradually. In fact, abdominal work can be done daily in your home.

157

A–1: Incline Sit-Up *(above)*
The inclined sit-up is performed
by bringing your knees up until
your legs are bent at a 90° angle
while your feet are in contact
with the bench or floor. Touch
your elbows to the knees while
keeping your hands together
behind your head.

B1: Twisting Incline Sit-Up

On an incline board with your hands behind your head, raise yourself, twisting as you come to a position three-quarters of the way up. The twist strengthens your obliques. This is also a stretching exercise for warm-up.

C1: Leg Raise *(below)*
Raise your legs approximately 2 feet and then bring them down slowly. Do not touch them to the floor. You should do a minimum of 50 raises without stopping.

D1: Bench Sit-Up *(right)*
With your legs over a low bench and your body crunched up as close as you can get, hold your hands behind your neck and raise up as high as you can toward the bench. You will only move a little, but this can be the best abdominal exercise of them all.

E1: Hanging Frog *(left)*
Hang straight down from the
bar using a shoulder-width grip.
Attempt to bring your knees to
your chest, but don't be disap-
pointed if you can't do it completely. It will probably take
you a few weeks before you can
bring the knees all the way up
to the chest.

F1: Hanging Leg Raise
hang from the bar with your legs together, and then bring your legs to a parallel position with the ground. Try to keep your legs perfectly straight.

G1-2: Jack Knife *(right)*
The jack-knife is a combination of a sit-up and a leg raise. With your arms outstretched and your legs kept stiff, raise your back and legs so that your hands touch your ankles.

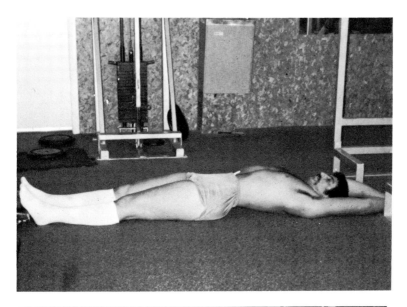

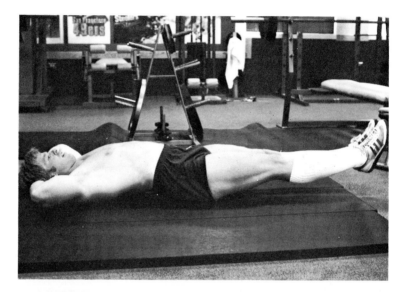

H1-2: Lying Knee Raise
This exercise greatly works your lower abdominals. Lie on your back with your hands behind your neck and bring your knees up toward your chest while bending your legs.

I1–2: Knee Raise
Rest your elbows on the pads and simply pull your knees up, bending your legs as you proceed. Try to bring your knees to your chest.

J1–2: Roman Chair Angle Sit-Up

Lie face up on the Roman chair. Then raise up from the bottom position to the top at an angle, twisting as you go up. In addition to working your abdominals, you will also work your obliques.

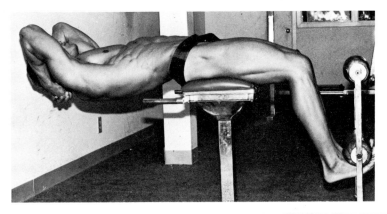

K1-2: Roman Chair Sit-up

With your body in this same position, sit up on the Roman chair with your hands behind your neck. Slowly extend yourself backwards until you are almost touching the floor. Then raise yourself up to the seated position. This exercise will also work your lower back.

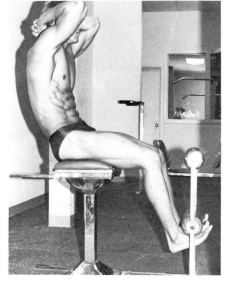

L1-2: Rope Abdominal Crunch
While kneeling on the floor, grasp the cable handles, pulling away at an angle of about 30° to 40°. Hold the cable close to your head and bend down till your head almost touches the floor. Do not move your arms.

M1-2: Bar Twist *(above)*
This exercise has many different purposes. It can be used to warm up, get the blood flowing, and loosen up the back and stomach. Hold the bar behind your head and twist from side to side. It will tighten up the abdominals and obliques. Do about 150 of these twists to warm up properly.

N1: Side Bend
Use a light dumbbell — 10
pounds or less — to work the
oblique muscle group. Bend to
the opposite side of the weight a
minimum of 50 times a side.
Don't use too heavy a weight, or
you'll bulk the muscle more than
you want to.

WEIGHT-CONDITIONING ROUTINES

General Fitness
Beginning Weight-Training Program

Do the following every other day, 3 days weekly. During the first week of training, do just 1 set of each exercise; the second week, do 2 sets; and in the third week, you can do all the recommended sets.

1. 1 set of leg extensions (**Legs A**), 12 reps.
2. 1 set of leg curls (**Legs C or D**), 12 reps.
3. 3 sets of squats (**Legs K**): use a very light weight (50 percent of what you estimate your maximum) for the 1st set, 12 reps.; on the 2d and 3d sets, do 75 percent of maximum, 8 reps. Avoid this exercise if you have knee problems until you consult with a doctor.
4. 1 set of donkey toe raises (**Legs R**), 10 burning reps. (start counting only after the burning begins).
5. 3 sets of flat flies (**Chest H**), 12 reps.
6. 3 sets of dumbbell incline presses (**Chest C**), 8–12 reps.
7. 3 sets of lat pulldowns (**Back E**), 12 reps., or chin-

ups (**Back J** or **Deltoids D**) if you can do at least 10.

8. 3 sets of seated military presses (**Deltoids F**), preferably with dumbbells, 8–12 reps.
9. 3 sets of curls (any kind in the **Arms & Wrists** section), 8 reps.
10. 3 sets of tricep extensions (**Arms & Wrists A** or **D**), 8– reps., or if you have no elbow problems, straight dips (**Arms & Wrists C**).
11. 1 set of hyperextensions (**Back M**), 20 reps. (if you have no lower-back problems).

General Fitness
Intermediate Weight-Training Program
(after 1 year, if you are up to it)
(This is actually a bodybuilding program.)

Do the following twice a week, either Monday or Thursday or Tuesday and Friday. You need two complete days to rest the muscle groups used.

1. 1 set of leg extensions (**Legs A**), 12 reps.
2. 1 set of leg curls (**Legs C or D**), 12 reps.
3. 5 sets of squats (**Legs K**): use a very light weight for the 1st set, 12 reps.; on 2nd set, do 67 percent of maximum, 10 reps.; on 3rd through 5th sets, do 75 percent of maximum, 12 reps.
4. 3 sets of donkey toe raises (**Legs R**), at least 10 burning reps.
5. 3 sets of chin-ups (**Back J** or **Deltoids D**), if you can do at least 10, or lat pulldowns (**Back E**), 12 reps.
6. 3 sets of shrugs (**Back A**), 12 reps.
7. 3 sets of T-bar rows (**Back H**), 12 reps., or bent-over parallel rows (**Back F**), 12 reps.
8. 3 sets of straight barbell curls (**Arms & Wrists L**), 8–12 reps. (make sure you keep your back straight).
9. 3 sets of dumbbell incline curls (**Arms & Wrists K**), 8–12 reps.
10. 2 sets of hyperextensions (**Back M**), 20 reps (avoid if you have lower-back problems).

Do the following on Tuesday and Friday or Monday and Thursday (alternately with the above routine).

1. 5 sets of bench presses (**Chest A**): 1st set at 50 percent of maximum, 12 reps.; 2nd set at 67 percent of maximum, 10 reps.; 3rd through 5th sets at 75 percent of maximum, 8 reps.
2. 3 sets of dumbbell incline presses (**Chest C**), 8 reps.
3. 3 sets of flat flies (**Chest H**), 12 reps.
4. 3 sets of dumbbell presses (**Deltoids G**), 8–12 reps.
5. 3 sets of bent-over lateral raises (**Deltoids B**), 8–12 reps.
6. 3 sets of tricep extensions (**Arms & Wrists A** or **D**), 8–12 reps.
7. 3 sets of tricep pushdowns (**Arms & Wrists I**) 8–12 reps.
8. 3 minutes of bench sit-ups (**Abdominals D**) or abdominal crunches (**Abdominals L**).

Bodybuilding

Advanced General Fitness Weight-Training Program
(This should be used only if you are really interested in bodybuilding and have lifted weights for at least 2 years.)

Do the following twice a week, either on Monday and Thursday or Tuesday and Friday. You need two complete days to rest these muscle groups.

1. Warm-up with various stretching routines.
2. 3 sets of leg extensions (**Legs A**), 12 reps., compounded with 3 sets of squats (**Legs K**), 12 reps. Do 1st set of leg extensions, then quickly do the 1st set of squats.
3. 3 sets of leg curls (**Legs C or D**), 12 reps., compounded with 3 sets of back squats (**Legs N**), 12 reps.
4. 3 sets of donkey toe raises (**Legs R**), at least 10 burning reps.
5. 3 sets of seated toe raises, at least 10 burning reps.
6. 3 sets of lat pulldowns (**Back E**), 12 reps., com-

pounded with 3 sets of T-bar rows (**Back H**), 12
reps. Do 1 set of pulldowns, then 1 set of T-bars
without rest; then rest for 2 minutes and continue.
7. 3 sets of cable rows to the chest (**Back I**), 12 reps.
8. 3 sets of upright rows (**Back B**), 12 reps.
9. 3 sets of supinating curls (**Arms & Wrists O**), 12
reps., compounded with 3 sets of pronating curls
(**Arms & Wrists P**), 12 reps.
10. 3 sets of straight barbell curls (**Arms & Wrists L**),
12 reps., supersetted with 3 sets of reverse curls
(**Arms & Wrists U**), 12 reps.
11. 2 sets of good-morning exercises (**Back N**), 12
reps. (do only if you have no lower-back problems).
12. 50 incline sit-ups (**Abdominals A**), 50 Roman chair
sit-ups (**Abdominals K**), 50 side bends (**Abdominals N**), 50 hanging leg raises (**Abdominals
F**), and 50 crunches (**Abdominals L**).

Do the following on Tuesday and Friday or Monday and
Thursday (alternately with the above routine).

1. Warm-up with various stretching routines.
2. 3 sets of flat flies (**Chest H**), 12 reps., supersetted
with 3 sets of bench presses (**Chest A**), 8 reps. *Immediately* after doing a set of flies, do a set of
presses (this is utilizing the pre-exhaust theory,
pre-exhausting the pecs with the flies before doing
the bench press, which is a compound exercise
working the pecs, delts, and triceps).
3. 3 sets of dumbbell decline presses (**Chest D**), 12
reps., supersetted with 3 sets of dumbbell incline
presses *(Chest C)*, 12 reps. This is also utilizing the pre-
exhaust method.
4. 3 sets of bent-over lateral raises (**Deltoids C**), 8
reps., supersetted with 3 sets of seated and standing dumbbell presses (**Deltoids G**), 8 reps.
5. 3 sets of easy-curl pullovers (**Chest E**), 8 reps.,
supersetted with 3 sets of close-grip tricep presses
(**Arms & Wrists E**), 8 reps. The presses are ac-
complished by holding the bar with your hands
close together, then pressing the bar straight up as

in a close-grip bench press: 8 reps. of this combination equals 1 set.
6. 3 sets of tricep kicks (**Arms & Wrists G**), 12 reps.
7. 3 sets of French curls (**Arms & Wrists B**), 12 reps.
8. 50 hanging frogs (**Abdominals E**), 50 Roman-chair
   angle sit-ups (**Abdominals J**), 50 bench sit-ups (**Abdominals D**), and 50 jack knives (**Abdominals G**).

Distance Running

Do this program every other day, 3 days weekly.

1. 1 set of leg extensions (**Legs A**), 12 reps.
2. 1 set of leg curls (**Legs C or D**), 12 reps.
3. 3–5 sets of squats (**Legs K**). The 1st year do just 3
   sets; after that do 5. 1st set, using very light
   weight, 20 reps.; 2nd set at 60 percent of maximum, 20 reps.; 3rd through 5th sets at 67 percent
   of maximum, 18 reps. Do these squats only twice
   a week.
4. 3 sets of pullovers (**Chest E**), 20 reps. Do only 2
   sets the 1st year.
5. 3 sets of donkey-toe raises (**Legs R**), 10 burning
   reps. Do only 1 set the 1st year.
6. 3 sets of bench presses (**Chest A**): 1st set at 50 percent of maximum, 12 reps.; 2nd through 3rd sets
   at 60 percent of maximum, 12 reps.
7. 3 sets of lat pulldowns (**Back E**), 12 reps.
8. 3 sets of seated dumbbell presses (see **Deltoids G**),
   12 reps.
9. 3 sets of standing bar curls (**Arms & Wrists L**),
   15–18 reps.
10. 1 set of hyperextensions (**Back M**), 25 reps., and 1
    set of good-morning exercises (**Back N**), 25 reps.
    Avoid these exercises if you have lower-back
    problems.

Racquetball

Do this program every other day, 3 times weekly.

1. 1 set of leg extensions (**Legs A**), 12 reps.
2. 1 set of leg curls (**Legs C or D**), 12 reps.

3. 3 sets of squats (**Legs K**): 1st set at 50 percent maximum, 12 reps.; 2nd and 3rd sets at 75 percent of maximum, 10 reps.
4. 2 sets on ad-ab machine (**Legs F**), 20 seconds on the Hydra-Gym machine.
5. 3 sets of flat flies (**Chest H**), 12 reps.
6. 3 sets of dumbbell incline presses (**Chest C**), 12 reps.
7. 3 sets of lat pulldowns (**Back E**), 12 reps.
8. 3 sets of bent-over lateral raises (**Deltoids B**), 12 reps.
9. 1 set of supinating curls (**Arms & Wrists O**), 12 reps.
10. 1 set of pronating curls (**Arms & Wrists P**), 12 reps.
11. 1 set up and 1 set down of wrist curls (**Arms & Wrists Q**), 20 reps.
12. 1 set of hyperextensions (**Back M**), 25 reps. Consult your physician if you have a back problem.

Tennis

Do this program every other day, 3 times weekly, but never the day before a big match.

1. 1 set of leg extensions (**Legs A**), 12 reps.
2. 1 set of leg curls (**Legs C or D**), 12 reps.
3. 3 sets of squats (**Legs K**), or leg presses (**G, H, or I**), 12 reps. Consult your doctor if you have knee problems.
4. 3 sets of ad-ab machine (**Legs F**), 20 seconds on Hydra-Gym, or 2 sets to failure on Nautilus.
5. 3 sets of donkey-toe raises (**Legs R**), at least 10 burning reps.
6. 3 sets of pullovers (**Chest E**), 12 reps.
7. 3 sets of dumbbell incline presses (**Chest C**), 12 reps.
8. 3 sets of flat flies (**Chest H**), 12 reps.
9. 3 sets of lat pulldowns (**Back E**), 12 reps., or if you can do at least 3 sets of chin-ups (**Back E**), 12 reps., or, if you can do at least 3 sets of chin-ups (**Back J or Deltoids D**), for 10 reps, do them.

10. *After the 1st year,* add 3 sets of cable rows (**Back I**), 12 reps.
11. 1 set of supinating curls (**Arms & Wrists O**), 12 reps.
12. 1 set of pronating curls (**Arms & Wrists P**), 12 reps.
13. 1 set up and down of wrist curls (**Arms & Wrists R & S**), 20 reps.
14. 1 set of reverse curls (**Arms & Wrists T**), 12 reps.
15. 1 set of hyperextensions (**Back M**), 25 reps., or 1 set of good-morning exercises (**Back N**), 25 reps. Avoid if you have a back problem until you consult a physician, preferably a sports-medicine specialist.

Swimming

Do this program every other day, 3 days weekly, but never the day before a meet.

1. 1 set of leg extensions (**Legs A**), 12 reps.
2. 1 set of leg curls (**Legs C or D**), 12 reps.
3. 3 sets of squats (**Legs K**), 12 reps. Avoid if you have knee problems until you consult your physician.
4. 1 set of bar lunges (**Legs O**), 25 reps. Be careful if you have knee problems.
5. 3 sets of toe raises (**Legs S**), 10 burning reps.
6. 1 set of ad-ab machine (**Legs F**), 30 seconds on Hydra-Gym.
7. 3 sets of pullovers (**Chest E**), 20 reps.
8. 3 sets of flat flies (**Chest H**), 12 reps.
9. 3 sets of lat pulldowns (**Back E**), 12 reps.
10. 1 set of curls (any kind in **Arms & Wrists** section), 12 reps.
11. 1 set of reverse curls (**Arms & Wrists T**), 12 reps.
12. After the first year, do 100 sit-ups and 100 reps. various leg raises (**Abdominals C or F**).

Bicycling

Do this program every other day, 3 days weekly.
1. 1 set of leg extensions (**Legs A**), 12 reps.

2. 1 set of leg curls (**Legs C or D**), 12 reps.
3. 3 sets of squats (**Legs K**), 12 reps. Avoid if you have knee problems until you see a sports-medicine specialist.
4. 1 set of leg presses (**Legs G, H, or I**), 12 reps.
5. 1 set of bar lunges (**Legs O**), 25 reps.
6. 3 sets of donkey-toe raises (**Legs R**), 10 burning reps.
7. 3 sets of pullover (**Chest E**), 20 reps.
8. 3 sets of bench presses (**Chest A**), 12 reps.
9. 3 sets of chin-ups (**Back J or Deltoids D**), 10 reps. each, or 3 sets of pulldowns (**Back E**), 12 reps.
10. 3 sets of curls (any kind in the **Arms & Wrists**) section), 12 reps.
11. 1 set of reverse curls (**Arms & Wrists T**), 12 reps.
12. 1 set of hyperextensions (**Back M**), 25 reps.
13. 1 set of good-morning exercises (**Back N**), 25 reps.

HOW TO CHOOSE YOUR HEALTH CLUB

Choosing Your Club

Now that you are out of school, you don't have the luxury of free gyms, so its time to start thinking about selection of a facility that fulfills your needs. It can be confusing to sort through the many ads and sales pitches in choosing what I'll call your club. Several factors need to be considered. One club simply has an old-fashioned gym, some racquetball courts and a track; yet another just offers weight-lifting facilities. Which is right for you?

Preparation is necessary to make an intelligent club choice. You will spend hundreds of hours at your club, maybe thousands over the years, so put time into choosing—utilize your investigative skills. The number and types of abuses in the health club industry may further convince you to invest some effort. As a senior trial attorney for the Bureau of Consumer Protection in the Federal Trade Commission, I was shocked by the extensive fraud uncovered in the national health-spa investigation. Some of the tricks were the selling of lifetime memberships to seventy-year-olds, getting individuals drunk at champagne parties and then signing them up. Though the majority of abuses such as these have ended, you should still be on the lookout for unethical operators. A special note of warning: be wary of new clubs opening with very low, unrealistic membership charges. If it's not a national chain with a solid reputation like Holiday Health Spa, European, Vic Tanny or some other reputable company, be careful. Your red flag should go up if the operator is not a locally well-known person with a good reputation. Also, a common abuse

179

occurs when a new club is opened by a stranger to town. Ridiculously low charges like $50 a year are offered. After signing up a few hundred new members, the "club manager" and all the equipment disappear over the weekend. Such con artists may still roam for whom you should be on the lookout.

The first step in club selection is to decide what kind of facility you want. Do you want to combine your weight lifting with racquetball or swimming and running? Do you already belong to a country club or YMCA which has racquetball courts, tennis courts, swimming pool, and track? If you belong to such a club, then you shouldn't waste money on a membership to a huge facility that offers everything under one roof. I have found that you can get more out of the different sports by belonging to two or three clubs. For example, my YMCA membership extends me use of racquetball courts, swimming pool, track, and also a small weight room. I also have access to one of the best heavy-duty weight rooms in the state.

Therefore, I suggest initially making a list of the facilities that you want, in order of preference. Check into the cost of joining a weight-lifting gym, and either a YMCA or racquetball club for the racquetball privileges alone. You might combine the cost of a good weight-lifting club at about $150 a year, and either a $100 YMCA membership or a partial racquetball club membership for $120 a year. This is preferable because not only are you getting the best from each facility, but you are saving $100 a year in membership fees. Those gigantic facilities that offer racquetball, swimming, and numerous other activities besides weight lifting don't always have the best weight-lifting facility nor proper instruction. A lot of shiny Nautilus, Paramount or other expensive equipment doesn't ensure that the facility is of high quality nor that it is suitable for you. Remember, the type of equipment is not the most important reason for joining a club. You could be fit by running on your old school track and working out with neighbors in a garage equipped with an Olympic weight set, a few benches, and a squat rack.

The next important step is to look for clubs that have honest, quality management and qualified instructors. Call the Better Business Bureau to check if any complaints have been registered on a specific club. Call the local AAU chapter for recommendations. Ask local coaches if they send their boys to any particular gym. Probably the best method is to ask your friends about their clubs or their friends' clubs. If you are new to an area, ask your old club operator if he has any recommendations. If you didn't belong to a club in your previous home, or if you simply used your school's gym, you might talk to friends who have visited your new area in the past and worked out at a local club. Word of mouth is a good route to try.

After you have a list of potential clubs that fit the initial criteria, visit each one at your typical workout time to observe how crowded it is and what kind of attention the instructors are giving. Check the cleanliness of the facilities and the condition of the equipment. What are the members like? A club is more enjoyable if you are compatible with them.

Most importantly, beware of an extremely strong sales pitch. A good club doesn't need one. Observe the management and staff. Is the manager helpful? Does he show a real interest in helping you get in shape? Do the manager and instructors seem to know what they are talking about? Be alert to unbelievable claims about what they can do with your body. It is realistic to state you could lose two inches off your waist, lose ten pounds, add an inch on your arms and an inch to your chest in the first six weeks. However, to tell you that you will lose forty pounds, six inches off your waist, and add three inches on your arms and five inches to your chest in the first month is very unrealistic. The manager or instructor should suggest practical goals for you and be able to maintain good records of your progress. Additionally, does the manager have any awards or trophies for his club? Does he have a reputation in the field beyond the city or state? Do other clubs think highly of the club's management? (It doesn't hurt to ask each club what they think of each other.) Try to talk to some members for their opinion of the club, the management, and instructors. Ask a member if he has any complaints about the club.

The significance of joining a club with quality and experienced management is demonstrated by the story of Bob Pure's remarkable recovery under the skillful care of Rafael Guerrero, the managing owner of Gold Coast Gyms in Ft. Lauderdale, Florida. In 1975, Bob twisted his back climbing into a boat with scuba equipment on. The following morning he experienced lower-back pain, and two days later he had an extreme pain in his right lower calf area. An orthopedic physician x-rayed his lower back, diagnosed the problem as sciatica and prescribed traction in the hospital for two weeks. Bob refused the hospital stay and received ultrasound therapy. During the next eighteen months, he lived in constant pain, having become 85% immobile. Bob's right leg had atrophied one inch and he had developed a noticeable curve in his spine.

When Bob approached Rafael's gym for assistance, Rafael requested a complete diagnosis from the attending physician before he would allow Bob to start. After receiving this information, Rafael started Bob lying down on the carpet while holding his lower back and then having Bob lift each leg backward as high as possible. Then he had Bob perform sidebends to stretch his spine, followed by bench presses with his feet upon the bench. Rafael stayed with Bob an hour each workout and gradually had him begin hyperextensions using the Roman chair. Eventually, under Rafael's supervision, Bob added good-morning exercises, presses, inclines, curls, and leg work.

When Bob started he could only bench press forty pounds; he later benched 265 after about a year in the gym. Cases like Bob's have been occurring worldwide. Bob was fortunate that he joined a club that had as its manager-owner an individual as skilled and concerned as Rafael Guerrero.

Though not everyone has access to a gym with such high-quality management, almost every medium-to-large-sized city in the country has at least one good club with a competent, concerned staff. The large cities will most likely have a few really good clubs. By doing your homework you can find one in your area.

Of course, what you can afford will be an important consideration. For many of you, the cost factor will not be important; you are prepared to pay for the best. However, most people today must consider costs. As I noted earlier, the cost of the YMCA and the weight-lifting club could amount to $250 a year, but the cost of the huge, everything-under-one-roof club could cost from $350 to $550 yearly. On the other hand, if you are just beginning and are lucky enough to be near a YMCA that has good instruction, a well maintained and well equipped weight room, a pool, a track, and racquetball courts, joining the YMCA might be sufficient for your needs. After some progress you may want to become further involved in weight training. Then may be the time to join a heavy-duty weight-lifting club with capable instructors to train you.

The following list of guidelines will help you in your search for a club. Good luck!

GUIDELINES FOR PICKING OUT A CLUB

1. List all the facilities you want in your club.
2. List all the clubs in your immediate area that have the facilities for which you are looking.
3. Call the Better Business Bureau to see if there are any complaints about the club.
4. Call the local chapter of the AAU to see if any clubs in the area are recommended.
5. Call the local college. Either ask the strength coach (if there is one) or football coach for a recommendation. If no colleges are nearby ask some top high school's staff for advice.
6. Ask your friends if they belong to a club and what they recommend.
7. If you are new in town, ask your old friends and your old club staff (if you belonged to one there) if they know anything about clubs in your new area.
8. Check to see if there are any national chains in your area. Do they have a good reputation nationally?

9. Do the local club owners have any state or national reputation? Does the local manager have a good reputation locally?
10. Are any of the staffs published? If so, read their books, their articles, or articles written about them.
11. What background do the managers and instructors have?
12. Do the staffs seem competent and concerned?
13. Are any of these clubs making a hard sales pitch or bloated promises? If they are, beware!
14. Do you like the members? Are you compatible with them?
15. Ask some members what they really think about their club and staffs.
16. Ask the clubs what they think about each other.
17. Are the facilities clean and is the equipment well maintained?
18. Check to see if the costs of your club or clubs' membership is worth what it provides for you and, obviously, is what you can afford.
19. Check to see if the club has won any awards.
20. Lastly, do you feel comfortable in that club? You want a club that fits your exercise needs but also makes you want to be there, instead of causing you to feel anxious and make you want to run out as soon as you get there.

INDEX

This book has been designed to allow the user to find specific exercises quickly. The right running head (top of the right-hand page) has the chapter names in boldface type. If an exercise appears on that page or the adjacent left-hand page, the exercise letter designation will appear next to the boldface name. Thus, **Deltoids A-B** at the top would indicate that the first two deltoid exercises (in this case, the front deltoid raise and the bent-over lateral raise) appear on the indicated pages. By quickly thumbing through the book, the reader can easily find the exercise he wishes. The index below, therefore, gives the chapter name and letter instead of the page numbers, as is more common in indexes.

Other great training books!

Shape Up for Soccer

by Rich Hunter (Notre Dame soccer coach) & Pete Broccoletti
100s of photos, approx. 224 pp., 6½" x 8½", index, clothbound $14.95, wirebound
$9.95

The **only** total conditioning book for the world's most popular sport (the fastest-growing sport in North America).

Coach Rich Hunter's program was called "the best in the nation" by U.S. National Team Coach Walt Chyzowych. And now it is available to everyone.

The program is geared to soccer players at all levels from age 12 to adult. Beginning with the all-important stretching exercises, the program's principal sections include comprehensive exercise routines in running, speed development, inside and outside ball exercises, weight training, skill development, plus special sections on nutrition for soccer players, goalkeeper exercises, youth conditioning, and appendixes in skill evaluation, indoor and outdoor drills, and sample practice schedules.

The Notre Dame Weight-Training Program for Football

by Pete Broccoletti, with Pat Scanlon
180 photos, 160 pp., 6½" x 8½", index, wirebound $9.95

This book is in a class by itself, and its excellent reception from coaches throughout the country proves it. After an initial discussion of nutrition and flexibility exercises, the first part of the text contains exercises by body part; the second part contains specifically designed in- and off-season weight routines by position played on the field.

The Notre Dame Weight-Training Program for Baseball, Hockey, Wrestling, & Your Body

by Pete Broccoletti with Pat Scanlon
222 photos, 216 pp. 6½" x 8½", index, clothbound $14.95, wirebound $9.95

The most complete, straightforward program ever devised for the baseball, wrestling, or hockey player or body builder. The book starts with comprehensive nutrition and flexibility chapters; then it proceeds to give 122 weight exercises, broken down by body part, and then in- and off-season weight routines by sport and (in the case of baseball) by position played. The body-building routines include programs for beginning, intermediate, and advanced students.

Building Up!
The Young Athlete's Guide to Weight Training

by Pete Broccoletti
110s of photos! Spiral binding so you can work with an open book!
192 pp. 6½" x 8½" clothbound $14.95, wirebound $9.95

This is **the** training manual for 12-to-17-year-olds. Specifically designed for growing bodies. Top advice about nutrition and health. Exercises by body part (including body flexibility). Weight conditioning routines keyed to football, basketball, baseball, soccer, swimming, and bodybuilding. Coach's checklist. Player's checklist. Index of all exercises.

Coupon on next page
Available at your bookseller, or order direct

RIP-OUT COUPON

ICARUS PRESS, P.O. Box 1225, South Bend, IN 46624

Please rush me the following books:

_____ copies *35 & Holding: Complete Conditioning for the Adult Male*
_____ Clothbound $16.95 _____ Wirebound $10.95

_____ copies *Shape Up for Soccer* _____ Clothbound $14.95 _____ Wirebound $9.95

_____ copies *The Notre Dame Weight-Training Program for Football*
_____ Wirebound $9.95

_____ copies *Building Up, The Young Athlete's Guide to Weight Training*
_____ Clothbound $14.95 _____ Wirebound $9.95

_____ copies *The Notre Dame Weight-Training Program for Baseball,*
Hockey, Wrestling, & Your Body
_____ Clothbound $14.95 _____ Wirebound $9.95

Name _____

Street _____

City/state/zip _____

_____ Payment enclosed _____ VISA _____ Master Charge

_____ Acc't no. _____ Exp. _____

Indiana residents please add sales tax.